Including Children with Cerebral Palsy in the Early Years Foundation Stage

Written by
Lindsay Brewis

with a personal statement from
Kayleigh Black

Illustrated by
Martha Hardy

371.9046
BRE

Published 2008 by A&C Black Publishers Limited
38 Soho Square, London W1D 3HB
www.acblack.com

First published 2008 by Featherstone Education Limited

ISBN 978-1-9060-2922-7

Text © Lindsay Brewis 2008
Illustrations © Martha Hardy 2008

A CIP record for this publication is available from the British Library.

Printed in **Malta by Gutenberg Press Limited**

This book is produced using paper that is made from wood grown in
managed, sustainable forests. It is natural, renewable and recyclable.
The logging and manufacturing processes conform to the environmental
regulations of the country of origin.

To see our full range of titles
visit **www.acblack.com**

Contents

Introduction and how to use this book

The Early Years Foundation Stage (EYFS) covers the first 60+ months of a child's life. For all children this is a period of rapid growth and development from a baby who, though physically dependent, is already a resilient, capable learner, to an independent child ready to set off on a school career. The EYFS focuses on the excitement of this journey of discovery. It provides practitioners with the inspiration, practical guidance and guiding principles to help and support the child.

The six areas of learning and development of the EYFS

- Personal Social and Emotional Development
- Communication Language and Literacy
- Problem Solving, Reasoning and Numeracy
- Knowledge and Understanding of the World
- Physical Development, and
- Creative Development

bring together the principles and themes of the previous *Guidance for the Foundation Stage* and *Birth to Three Matters*. The EYFS guidance also includes the *National Standards for Under 8s Daycare and Childminding*.

This is good news for children with cerebral palsy. It enables practitioners to access guidance appropriate to the child's needs at every developmental stage from birth to five years in each area of learning, irrespective of their chronological age. The Practice Guidance for the EYFS is clear and evidenced based. The guidance understands the importance of partnership working and a multi-agency approach.

This book is packed with practical advice and ideas that really work. They acknowledge that professional advice will be needed for some children, and signpost when and where to find more support.

Putting Principles into Practice

There is a clear expectation in the EYFS 'Putting Principles into Practice' that a diverse range of children with different needs and abilities from different backgrounds should be included. This book will help you work with the curriculum guidance and give the child with cerebral palsy opportunities to join in and be spontaneous. Children with cerebral palsy will need your help and ingenuity to ensure they get lots of opportunities to play and become sociable. This book will give you hints and tips, as well as examples of good practice in the way adult support can enrich the experiences for the child.

One of the challenges for practitioners is understanding what it means to grow up and live with cerebral palsy, and we are indebted to Kayleigh Black for sharing her experiences with us. Readers can also follow the parents' journey described in Working with Parents (see page 29). This will help practitioners to take parents' and carers' feelings and anxieties into account in meeting the child's needs, and brings home dramatically the almost overwhelming number of professionals the parent must deal with.

This book can help you make the most of the EYFS for young children with cerebral palsy. It will:

Inform you about:

- the different types of cerebral palsy and how they affect children's movements;
- how cerebral palsy affects children in a very wide variety of ways;
- how the family may be feeling;
- how the child might feel and how this affects their later life;
- who the other professionals working with the family are, and how they can help you.

Support you by:

- helping you contribute to the multi-agency team working with the family;
- offering tips on different approaches;
- giving many examples of good practice;
- providing guidance on adapting the physical environment;
- giving ideas for observing and recording progress.

Inspire you by:

- giving you examples of real children succeeding in real settings;
- providing lots of practical ideas for play;
- showing how to get the best out of dual placements;
- suggesting many practical activities that fit with the EYFS framework.

Make you think about:

- how the child with cerebral palsy can be helped to communicate and participate;
- how families interact with all the different professionals and our role in bringing all the different strands together;
- the special issues for brothers and sisters of children with cerebral palsy.

Make you ask yourself some hard questions such as:

- How does it feel to be a child growing up with cerebral palsy?
- How can I use risk assessment to ensure the child participates and is not left out?
- How can I use the understanding I gain to support all the children in the group?

Links to the EYFS framework and the Early Support materials

The EYFS framework is a detailed and practical guide to meeting both statutory and good practice requirements for early years providers and practitioners. The framework is based on the *Every Child Matters* principles and organised in themes, which are designed to be inclusive of all children. The guidance with the EYFS framework is backed up by detailed practical advice on CD-ROM and gives examples of meeting diverse needs.

Practitioners familiar with the Stepping Stones will find much of this still embedded in the Development Matters column of the practical guidance. These are now set out in age appropriate sections and it is important for practitioners to look through earlier developmental stages to find ways in which some children with cerebral palsy will be able to interact and respond. For example a child might be aged 48 months and the guidance will suggest that children at this age are usually developing 'independence in exploring activities' (Personal, Social and Emotional development). However a child with cerebral palsy may have difficulty with movement and communication and fewer opportunities to explore independently, and might be responding at the developmental stage of 8-20 months and be 'exploring the environment with interest'.

The EYFS framework accepts that no child develops uniformly across all areas of learning and expects that the profile of the child's learning will reflect individual and unique differences.

An excellent source of additional information and advice is the Early Support website http://www.earlysupport.org.uk/. Although the site deals exclusively with the needs of children under three, much of the free guidance material on individual disabilities has been written by experts in their fields and is suitable for a wider age range. There is specialist information, including information about cerebral palsy, in the 'For Families' section. You can read this yourself  and encourage parents to get their free copy if they have not already obtained one from their health visitor. There are Early Support booklets helping parents find childcare and explore their entitlement to benefits, all written in plain English. There are plans to make these materials available in languages other than English, so keep an eye on the site for future developments.

Help and support for parents and professionals is also available through the charity Scope. Response workers have access to the telephone service 'Language Line' and can arrange support for parents through translators in a range of languages. For information about cerebral palsy or access to translation please phone Scope Response on 0808 800 3333, email response@scope.org.uk or visit the Scope website www.scope.org.uk.

HemiHelp (www.hemihelp.org.uk/) is a UK charity for children and young people with hemiplegia and their families. HemiHelp can provide information about the condition and will tailor support for families and professionals. Their website contains fact sheets and other information, and they offer a helpline on 0845 123 2372.

Children with cerebral palsy may have a range of other learning disabilities such as hearing impairment, visual impairment or interaction difficulties on the autistic continuum. The Early Support materials for parents include a number of disabilities and contain a great deal of information to support children with multiple impairments.

First steps in making this book work for you

1. Read the opening pages giving you Key Facts (see page 10). This will answer many of the questions commonly asked by practitioners.
2. Take a little time to get to know the child. His or her parents may have a record book that they are happy to share with you. Some will have made a communication passport giving details of the way the child communicates, their likes and dislikes. Some families will already have reports from professionals and specialist groups they attend. Read through whatever the parents can give you and begin to understand the journey they have made so far.
3. Read the information in the section Working with Parents (see page 29). It will help you to understand the needs of the family.
4. If you can mange it, visit the parents at home and watch how the child enjoys the company of parents, friends and siblings. Observe how he engages with toys or music or words. Ask some of the questions you still need to have answered. Some parents will still be at the stage in their journey where they want to tell the new listener all the details of their child's life; others will be worn out with having told it so many times before. Be sensitive to this. If they are willing to share their story, listen actively and show interest and empathy. Most parents do not want sympathy but they do want others to understand.
5. Most children with cerebral palsy have contact with a large number of professionals and many attend specialist as well as universal settings. You will want to look at the sections on multi-agency work (page 44) and dual placements (page 48) as these will give you ideas for how you can all come together to support the child and family.

6. Dip in and out of this book to look at curriculum matters and play ideas. Use these to inspire you to take play and learning forward. Look at the useful addresses and websites for further ideas and resources. Read Kayleigh Black's account of one person's life with cerebral palsy and how exciting this can be. Most of all enjoy having this child in your group, and look forward to all the fun and laughter and the achievements you will share.

Everyone's different

Amy has a weakness on the left side of her body and struggles to keep up with the others when they run and play. Tom uses an electric wheelchair and a box that speaks for him. Both children have been affected by the condition known as cerebral palsy. Both children attend their local pre-school and both are making friends and progressing in their play, communication and learning.

Cerebral palsy is an umbrella term for a **non-progressive impact in the brain which affects movement, posture and coordination.** These problems may be seen at or around the time of birth or may not become obvious until early childhood. Cerebral palsy is a wide-ranging condition and can affect people in many different ways. No two people with cerebral palsy are affected in the same way.

If a person has cerebral palsy it means that the part of the brain which controls muscles and movement has been affected. Other areas of the brain may also be involved, affecting, for example, vision, communication, behaviour and learning.

In cerebral palsy the brain impairment is non-progressive, that is, it does not get worse or improve. However, the effects on the body may become more (or, sometimes, less) obvious as time goes by.

Key facts and questions answered

Who may have cerebral palsy?

Cerebral palsy is more common than generally realised. About one in every 400 children is affected, which means about 1,800 babies are diagnosed with cerebral palsy in Great Britain each year. This is about the same as children with visual (or hearing) impairments.

Types of cerebral palsy

Cerebral palsy affects the messages sent between the brain and the muscles. There are three types of cerebral palsy:

- spastic
- athetoid (or dyskinetic)
- ataxic .

They generally relate to the part of the brain that has been affected. The effects of cerebral palsy vary enormously from one person to another, with some people having a combination of two or more types.

Spastic cerebral palsy

'Spastic' means 'stiff' and this form of cerebral palsy causes the muscles to stiffen and decreases the range of movement in the joints. It is the most common form of cerebral palsy and occurs in three-quarters of people with the condition. The messages in the brain get changed so that the muscles are told to tighten but not to relax appropriately. Spasticity creates tightness in the muscles and a decreased range of movement in the joint. It can affect different areas of the body and may have an effect on speech.

Generally someone with spastic cerebral palsy has to work hard to walk or move. If the person is only affected on one side of their body the term used to describe this is 'hemiplegia'. If their legs are affected but their arms are unaffected or only slightly affected this is known as 'diplegia'. If both arms and both legs are equally affected, then the term used is 'quadriplegia'.

The spasticity in muscle groups resists attempts to pull limbs into place and children with spastic muscles need to be supported to move gradually to get their arms towards toys and equipment.

Athetoid (or dyskinetic) cerebral palsy

Children with athetoid cerebral palsy make involuntary movements because their muscle tone changes rapidly from floppy and loose to tense and still in a way they cannot control. Their speech can be hard to understand as they may have difficulty controlling the tongue, breathing and vocal cords. Hearing problems are also common in conjunction with athetoid cerebral palsy.

Children with athetosis are rarely still - they have too much movement; as soon as they try to initiate a movement or thought their body will start to move. In other words effort of any sort will increase athetosis. For children the problems of eye and hand coordination can be very severe. Some children will need to twist their body to get eye contact with a toy or equipment and then twist again to get their hand or arm to the item. For these children one attempt may be all they can achieve as asking them to repeat an action causes higher levels of involuntary movement.

Ataxic cerebral palsy

Children with ataxic cerebral palsy find it very difficult to balance. They may also have poor spatial awareness, which means it is difficult for them to judge their body position relative to other things around them. Ataxia affects the whole body. Most people with ataxic cerebral palsy can walk but they will probably be unsteady. They may also have shaky hand movements and irregular speech.

For children the problems of hand control mean that the child may need to keep toys and equipment close to their body as they play and explore materials.

Mixed

Children with cerebral palsy do not always fit nicely into the above descriptions. Children often have a mixture of symptoms, for example athetosis with ataxia, athetosis with spasticity and so on.

Handling a child with cerebral palsy

This section is about how you lift, carry, hold, and position a child and learn to control any muscle stiffness or uncontrolled muscle movements. Obviously the best way to handle a baby or young child depends on age, type of cerebral palsy and how the body is affected.

Here are some practical suggestions, by no means exhaustive:

- Try not to move the child suddenly or jerkily. The muscles may need time to respond to changes in position.
- Some children's muscles tense (spasm). Let muscles tense and relax in their own time - don't force movements.
- Fear can make muscle spasms worse, so give the child as much support as he needs when you are handling him, being careful not to give him more support than he needs.
- Whatever his size or level of impairment, make sure that the child spends time in different positions.
- Try to position the child so he can see what is going on around him.
- Many physically disabled children are greatly advantaged by properly fitting and supportive seating. As a general rule feet should be flat on the floor, knees bending at right angles, with hips firmly against the back of the seat. Some children benefit from chairs with arms. (See pages 81-83 for details of suppliers).
- A Dycem mat under the feet or to sit on can help keep the child in a safe position (see pages 81-83 for details of suppliers).
- Some children are particularly sensitive to losing their centre of gravity during rapid growth spurts and they can become clumsier and may be more disorganised.

Physiotherapists and occupational therapists will advise on the appropriateness of any arrangement for an individual child. They may need to show staff how to handle or carry a child in a way that will help him develop the best possible control over his body, and prevent back strain or injury.

Changing clothes

Getting dressed or changing clothes can sometimes be difficult for children with cerebral palsy. It is likely that parents will already have discovered the practicalities of loose, comfortable clothing. Velcro and elastic can be easier to manage than buttons and zips.

Toilet training

Establish a toilet training routine (unless told otherwise). Delay in toilet training is usually not because of medical factors but is more likely to result from a lack of opportunity/experience. However, toilet training may be more difficult for a child with cerebral palsy. For example, it may be hard for him to relax or use his muscles to empty his bowels. Continence can sometimes be a problem too. A therapist or health visitor can give help and support. (See pages 81-83 for sources of help and advice.)

Learning difficulties associated with cerebral palsy because of the impact in the brain may be seen in all types of cerebral palsy, including hemiplegia.

Cerebral palsy has an impact on the brain. The consequence of this is that part of the brain is injured. When this happens, research has shown that the brain tries to reconnect around the injured areas. This research, undertaken at the Brain and Behaviour Clinic at the Royal Maudsley Hospital (Robert Goodman (1998), Journal of Child Psychology & Psychiatry, Vol. 39, No. 3, pp. 347-354, Cambridge University Press) has shown that several things occur when the brain attempts to repair itself.

Most of these incidents occur before birth or during the first few years of life. This often has the following effects:

- The developing brain seems to value movement and will try to reconnect movement functions.
- The part of the brain available to make these new routes is the visual processing part and children therefore commonly have visual/spatial problems, even when sight itself is not affected.

- The developing brain will also commonly try to reconnect language functions. In trying to make new connections there will be several or many attempts ending in blind alleys or connecting with the wrong part of the brain. Many of these attempts will route through to the deepest parts of the brain where emotion and reactions are generated.
- A common reaction is to panic, the instant discharge of adrenalin into the system causing the 'fight or flight' response. This response is not under the child's control and may be triggered by very ordinary sights, sounds or smells. The research mentioned above found that 61% of children with hemiplegic cerebral palsy in the very large study had anxiety and conduct disorders, the most common being panic and oppositional behaviours. MRI scans, that track the way the brain reacts when active, enabled researchers to study this in detail.
- Other forms of cerebral palsy show the same levels of anxiety and conduct disorders and have the same increased tendency to panic.
- It has been noted by consultants in neurodisability that children with these difficulties are seen to have specific problems with the spatial concepts and can have difficulties with the operations that underpin mathematical knowledge and skills.
- While language is often preserved at the expense of spatial awareness the reconnection activity can cause difficulties with word finding and answering direct questions, and these can interfere greatly with demonstrating learning.
- Use pictures to support retrieval of knowledge; or cue in the speech with a simple starter sentence that begins to talk about an event, idea or area but is not completed, inviting the child to finish it; for example, 'Yesterday we talked about mountains and we said that mountains are ... ' The child may be able to insert the right word even when not able to answer the direct question 'Are mountains high or low?'.

The important thing is to keep searching for ways the child can demonstrate learning rather than keep hoping that one day they get it right! Differentiation and individual solutions, enabling children to record and demonstrate their learning are the key.

What other learning needs are associated with cerebral palsy?

While many children with cerebral palsy have no associated disorders, there are several linked conditions that could affect the child's ability to learn.

- Around 30% of children with cerebral palsy will have mild or moderate learning difficulties. This is more common in children with spastic quadriplegia. (The figure is around 15% when looking at all children.)
- Epilepsy will affect about 50% of children with cerebral palsy, although this will be well controlled in most cases. About half of all children who have epilepsy will also experience night time seizures. This can have a significant effect on their readiness to learn. All the medicines commonly taken to control epilepsy have some side-effects. Some of these side effects can also affect learning and behaviour.
- Many children with cerebral palsy have great difficulty eating enough food to promote healthy growth and well-being. Children may come to school hungry and may be unable to eat enough food at mealtimes to sustain them throughout the day. Many children with cerebral palsy actually need to eat more food than others of their age. This is always made worse if the child has a long journey to get to the setting. Snack breaks will be needed to top up energy levels for some children.
- Many children with cerebral palsy have impaired vision, often with a squint in one or both eyes. This can lead to visual processing difficulties. The child with a squint will receive two separate images for their brain to process and this can lead to difficulties perceiving the movement of people around. In an effort to correct this, some children with a squint, also called strabismus, will have their good eye patched to give the weaker eye more work to do and hopefully improve the muscle strength in that eye.

- Other visual impairments range from blindness to reduced ability to see line drawings. Every local authority will have access to an adviser in visual impairment and all settings should be able to seek advice from this service.
- When the insult to the brain which caused the cerebral palsy happened, the brain tried to repair itself. Before birth the brain wasn't using that part associated with visual processing, so the new pathways were routed through this area. This can lead to poor visual/spatial ability, even when vision is not  affected. Children with cerebral palsy may have difficulties organising spatial information if they cannot handle the objects. This can lead to difficulties with problem solving, reasoning and numeracy, and with spelling that are not related to the child's general ability.
- Hearing loss is a common feature of athetoid cerebral palsy and the poor posture and/or lung function of some children will lead to frequent infections which cause their ears to be congested and less able to hear.
- Some children with cerebral palsy have less ability to feel simple sensations like touch and pain. Other children are over sensitive to the touch of their clothes or to the textures of food.

Communication and speech difficulties

- Six out of ten children with cerebral palsy will have difficulties with language and communication. This figure rises where the child has athetoid cerebral palsy. The communication needs of children are a priority, as without a formal means of communication children will have huge difficulties with every aspect of their education.

- Formal systems may be sign, picture or word based and they can be simple sheets or books or electronic devices, depending on what suits the child. She will need lots of enjoyable opportunities to practise using communication every day in social as well as learning situations.

- Children with speech and language difficulties may not have had the opportunity to practise sentence structures or use a range of grammatical constructs. Scope has produced a reading pack to assist in teaching this small discrete group that takes a child through eye pointing activities to starting reading. (See pages 81-83.)

Anxiety and conduct disorders

The Brain and Behaviour Clinic at the Royal Maudsley Hospital undertook a study of a large number of children with hemiplegia (where one side of the body is more affected). HemiHelp has a useful factsheet on this. (See pages 81-83 for more information on HemiHelp.) Emotional and behavioural problems normally affect less than 10% of all children. However, the study found that more than 50% of children with hemiplegia showed difficulties in these areas. The children in the study came from stable homes and there were no obvious reasons for their behaviours.

- Because these difficulties are often caused by the neurological condition, they may not respond quickly to interventions.
- Families, as well as staff, may perceive these difficulties as part of poor parenting and this may make discussing difficulties awkward.
- These difficulties occur across all children with cerebral palsy, not just those with hemiplegia.
- The severity of the anxiety or oppositional behaviour is often not linked to the severity of the physical impairment and the children with the most need may get the least support.
- These behaviours do respond to positive behaviour management approaches, but because they can be entrenched they need a great deal of support to follow through with programmes. Support is through the educational psychology team or access to a clinical psychologist.

Autistic Spectrum Disorder (ASD)

There is an increased incidence of autistic spectrum disorders amongst children with cerebral palsy. Sometimes the behaviours that would allow clinicians to identify autism are masked by the physical difficulties. Children, whether severely affected, or ambulant and using their hands, may not be diagnosed as the ASD difficulties may be assumed to be 'normal' in cerebral palsy. Where communication and interaction difficulties are noted it is sensible to rule out autism as part of the cause. Keep a diary of behaviours that are causing concern and discuss them with the child's parents and with the Area SENCo. Following these discussions the family may want to seek the opinion of an educational psychologist.

Tiredness and determination

For the child with cerebral palsy there is always some, even considerable, physical effort required, whether it is the extra exertion needed to sit up in a chair or the demands made by trying to walk around.

Many children with cerebral palsy find it hard to listen and concentrate. Some may need to put extra effort into speaking or recording work. Children commonly do not understand that they are experiencing higher levels of fatigue and assume that others are just better at dealing with these levels of tiredness. They often persist with activities in order to fit in.

Sleep

Many children with cerebral palsy have difficulty sleeping, finding it hard to 'switch off' and only falling asleep when exhausted. Parents may be reluctant to discuss this because they feel others will judge them to be 'bad' parents in not establishing a sleep routine. If we all understand that this can be a problem for some children we can work together.

It is important to monitor fatigue levels and check on cross, tired behaviours at home. The child may smile in the setting but be poorly behaved and tearful once in the security of his own home.

More about hemiplegia

Hemiplegia is a condition affecting one side of the body (Greek hemi = half). It is often referred to as right or left-sided depending on the side of the body that is affected. Generally, injury to the left side of the brain will result in right hemiplegia and injury to the right side left hemiplegia.

Acquired hemiplegia results from damage to the brain during childhood. The most common cause is a stroke, but it can also result from an accident or infection. The causes of congenital hemiplegia are mostly unknown, and usually parents become aware of their child's hemiplegia gradually during his infancy.

The child is likely to show a weaker side and many children with hemiplegia become very good at using the stronger side and ignoring the weaker side. It is very important that the child learns to use the weaker side to the best possible level. Adults should encourage the child to sit with feet flat and bottom back and bring both hands up in front to handle and manipulate toys and equipment.

Two-wheeled push-along bikes can also encourage use of both sides as the child learns to push firmly through the weaker leg and steer using both arms.

The organisation HemiHelp offers information and support to children and young people with hemiplegia, their families and those working with them. They produce a wide range of fact sheets, many of which can be downloaded free from their website or you can get support by telephoning their Helpline. (See pages 81-83.)

Learning and playing with cerebral palsy

The ideas for play activities which follow can support the EYFS framework. The keys next to each activity show the areas that are relevant. For more detailed curriculum support see pages 53-71:

- Personal, Social and Emotional Development (PSE)
- Communication, Language and Literacy (CLL)
- Problem Solving, Reasoning and Numeracy (PRN)
- Knowledge and Understanding of the World (KUW)
- Physical Development (PD)
- Creative Development (CD).

Play is vital for all children. It is the way we explore the world about us and our place in it, offering opportunities to relax, express feelings, experience success and failure, learn about communication and our physical capacities.

Remember, toys themselves are not essential for play. Children will often get just as much enjoyment playing with the empty box that once housed a toy, or with plastic cartons or old clothes. The key word is FUN - something we can all offer to every child.

Word play (CLL) (CD)

Word play can take place when the adult is occupied with practical tasks such as setting up an activity. Nursery rhymes and stories can be personalised to include the child's name, family members, best friends, animals and interests. Rhymes such as 'Incy Wincy Spider' can grow in speed, volume and roughness with the child, to the level that he enjoys.

Even very young children enjoy absurdities and will have fun helping you make up funny stories about family members: for example, Gran speeding off in her Ferrari as she tries to outdo Lewis Hamilton! Repetition and predictability are just as important though!

Hand play (PRN, KUW, PD)

Bobbing and dipping

- Lay out a large plastic sheet. In a bowl of water add bath foam (one that suits the child) and encourage splashing, clapping, blowing, patting into shapes, smearing the bubbles on themselves, a mirror, you, plastic toys and so on.
- Fill a bowl with coloured water, jelly, or thin coloured cornflour paste. Add one or more of dried beans, lentils, sand or rice and encourage the child to squeeze and pat the mixture.

Objects that float (too big to swallow) and sink, fly and bounce

- Play with plastic toys, soaps, expanding sponges, sponge shapes, home-made shakers (clear plastic bottle filled with a few brightly coloured beads that whirl and rattle when patted).
- Explore sinking toys that dive when they gradually fill with water, objects that 'glug' as they sink.
- Blow bubbles for the child to pop or try to catch. Encourage an outstretched hand.

- In ball play try using a bigger ball so that the child is encouraged to use both hands.

Touching and shaking

- Sew small toys firmly on to the back of a pair of old gloves, cut to cover the wrist and fist with no finger holes. You can use any noisy or bright materials, make them dance or tell a story. Bells and other noise-making toys are available commercially, often on Velcro bands to fix to wrist or ankle (see pages 81-83 for suppliers).

Reading (CLL, PD)

Encourage the child to turn the pages of a book while reading. If you are using a picture book with stiff pages you can attach a cardboard tab with a piece of sponge stuck to it so that the child finds the pages easier to grasp.

Interactive toys (PRN, KUW, PD, CD)

The advantage of these is that the child gets an immediate result from their actions! There are many toys available in bigger stores and supermarkets that involve pressing a switch or pulling a lever to activate. Often we buy these toys and the child seems excited to play with them and then loses interest. The child will enjoy these toys more and for longer if you and other children share the excitement of the activity with them.

Playing with other children (PSE, CLL, PRN)

Playing with other children helps the child to practise sharing, taking turns, waiting for attention, listening and so on.

Very young children play alongside each other and only interact briefly.

However this is a shared play experience and adults supporting very young children often act as the bridge between them, pointing out shared areas of play and encouraging showing and sharing. Some children will need this adult support to play alongside other children for a longer period of time. As children mature they begin to take part in co-operative play.

Role play (CD, CLL, KUW)

Role play is very popular with young children. Sometimes children with cerebral palsy find themselves in less exciting roles and adult intervention may be needed to ensure that all the children experience a variety of roles. For example, give out hats to define positions or roles or engineer things so that the child takes on a more important role. For example, when playing shop, positioning a child behind the counter indicates to other children a shopkeeper role. You can adapt costumes so that they slip over anyone's head by cutting up the seams and making Velcro fastenings.

Early board games (PD, PRN, CLL)

Games of chance are very popular with young children as everyone in the group has the same chance to win. Small adaptations to the dice or playing pieces may help independent play, such as larger foam dice that can be dropped or thrown without fear of damage. Small, hand-shaped yoghurt drink pots can be painted to make easy-to-handle play pieces. Magnetised boards can help smooth play.

Floor games (PD, CLL, PRN, PSE, KUW)

Most young children love very physical games. Games involving rolling, tickling, crawling, pulling and pushing will appeal to a wide range of children. Young children are rarely as fragile as they look, and if there are no medical reasons why not, most children can join in. Remember that spasm and head control may limit the type of physical play a child can take part in. The child's parents and physiotherapist can advise you.

Sardines

You need three or more players. One child lies on a mat. Another child lies down as close as possible. The third child tries to get in the middle. Then one of the outer children tries to get in the middle. The winner is the one who stays in the middle most.

Logs

Each child lies on a mat. The other children roll the child to a marker. The child being rolled resists. The winner is the one that is most difficult to roll.

Happy feet

This game is played with bare feet. Children are paired and a way of moving is stated - rocking, bottom shuffling, walking on each other's feet etc. Move around the available space touching your feet to as many other pairs of feet as you can. You can set this at an appropriate level for the children and can use hands, elbows or shoulders for variety. Older children or adults can be involved as partners.

Start and stop

This version of statues puts the child with cerebral palsy 'in charge' of other children and adults. The child can use voice, cards held up or a talking switch to tell everyone else to start and stop movements. The child can be helped to choose the best statues to stay in the game, and spot moving statues to be eliminated.

Four in a bed

The child and three others lie on the floor on their backs with arms above their heads. They roll (with assistance if needed) while singing, "There were ten in the bed and the little one said, 'Roll over, roll over.'".

Play through sensory experience (PSE, CLL, KUW PRN)

Scope and RNIB Cymru have put together a series of curriculum linked activity cards. Contact earlyyears@scope.org.uk for an electronic copy. All children will enjoy these activities but they will be specially useful where children have very high support needs and/or additional sensory impairments.

Smell

If you plan to use essential oils as part of this sensory play, check carefully the dilutions required and instructions for their safe use and effects. Check for known allergies for all the children playing. There are many scratch and sniff products available. These are great fun but often have a short life span. In summer lying on your back and seeing and smelling petals can be much better. Cooking is a great way to experience smells. Offer the child a few spices to smell and ask which one should go into the mix. (You will know which ones to offer!) You might offer some really inappropriate ones to see what the reaction is!

Massage

From tiny babies, children enjoy the sensation of massage. Making this a playful experience can involve singing, rhymes and simple finger play. The scent used can help children prepare to be involved in these play activities. Older children will still enjoy hand and foot massage.

Messy mixing

Children like to create smells, good as well as noxious! Using household items that the child can handle safely, let the child mix up smelly potions. If the child cannot handle the items they can choose which ones are added, and be helped by another child or adult to do the mixing.

Sights (KUW, PD, PRN)

Shiny paper

Shiny paper can be cut and dangled to move in the breeze. Children can be involved in choosing or cutting the paper as appropriate. Sweet wrappers and tin foil also work well.

Lamps and lights

Most children enjoy watching fibre optic lights and lava lamps but lamps must be positioned away from the child as they get hot.

Small torches can be used to great effect in a darkened room. Cover the lamp with coloured film for more effects.

Catching the beam of the torch is a simple game that can be played with one or more than one child. The room is darkened and the children each have a paper in front of them. Each child has to 'catch' the light as it lingers in their own circle. The light is under the control of the adult who can adjust, as necessary, the length of time each child has to react.

Sounds (CD, CLL, KUW)

Most children love music and it may be fun to develop a tape or CD of each child's favourite music over a period of time.

Home-made and bought instruments that can be shaken, banged or blown are great fun. Even when the child cannot hold an instrument they may be able to have one attached with Velcro straps to their wrist or ankle. Banging saucepans and shaking beans in bottles can be as much fun as playing an expensive instrument.

Many electronic keyboards make a wide variety of sounds and require very little pressure to operate.

Touch (CD, KUW, CLL, PSE)

Some children may be wary of new textures. Be sensitive to this.

Feely box

The child touches (grasps) an object in a box where he cannot see the shape. This can be a game where the child tries to name the object, or an experience where the child experiences touch without vision. There could be a series of boxes with pairs of objects for matching games. (See *The Little Book of Treasure Baskets*, Featherstone Education 2002.)

What touched you?

Three objects, each with a distinctive feel, are placed on a tray. The tray is shown and the objects handled. The tray is removed, the child closes her eyes and the adult gently touches the child's bare skin with one of the objects. The child tries to work out which one it was.

Gardening (CLL, KUW, PSE)

Gardening can involve handling earth, making mud, digging with a spoon or hands, looking for mini beasts, smelling. A window box or plant tray will do if you don't have a garden.

Growing up with cerebral palsy

My name is Kayleigh. I am 19 years old and have just finished school and am waiting for my A level results. I hope to go to university to study journalism and media.

I am a bubbly and positive person who has cerebral palsy. I am a wheelchair user. I can use a keyboard slowly but prefer to dictate rather than write myself. I have a dog for the disabled, Vicky, who helps me in so many practical ways, taking off my night splints, picking stuff up for me and so on, but far more than that she is a great friend, good company and helps me to break the ice when meeting new people. They may not know what to say to me but they can always say hello to Vicky.

Before nursery I went with my mum to a special parent and baby group, one of Scope's schools for parents, and then went with support to my local nursery school. I loved nursery. I can remember the excitement of the water tray and making bubble and butterfly paint prints are some of my earliest memories. The staff were really great in my primary school. They always tried to find a way for me to be included and this was so important to me. There were times I was left out of play dates and parties and this hurt, made me feel isolated and has left me feeling that it takes a long time for me to trust other people.

The most important things the early years staff did for me were:
- giving me choices;
- not making assumptions;
- allowing me more time to respond;
- making chill out time and space;
- getting me a bike I could use outside with the other children (although this took a long time to arrange).

I would also have liked them to find more ways of including me especially in PE. I often found myself washing the paint pots instead of joining in. I also think that more could have been done to explain my difficulties to me and to the rest of the children. I think they just needed a really simple non-medical explanation and a chance to try out all my special equipment. Some of the children were jealous of the attention and opportunities I had, such as visiting the local special school every so often. I want to tell practitioners not to be afraid to make mistakes and always look for solutions.

I am lucky that when I go to university, I am going to get some voice recognition software for my computer to help me with my work and also a dyslexia assessment. It's a shame that I have had to wait so long - it would have been great to have access to some specialised resources and advice while still at school. So I would ask practitioners to please find out what is out there for children with cerebral palsy. There is so much that can be done to find new ways of making learning easier.

Sometimes having a one-to-one support worker was hard. It was too easy for this to get in the way of my friendships. Other children would ask the assistant, 'Can I do that with Kayleigh?' or 'Can I borrow Kayleigh's pencil?'. I felt invisible. Friends could also get frustrated by how long it took me to do things and I missed too many playtimes going to the toilet or getting dressed which takes me much longer than other people. I think that a lot more could be done to help children with cerebral palsy build friendships. I also think there should be a disabled character in the Harry Potter books. Perhaps I should write to JK Rowling.

I stayed in my local school all the way through my education and I am very glad of that. It has given me the chance to go to university, but the link with local disability organisations has enabled me to take up boccia (bowling for the disabled). This has opened so many doors for me. I am just back from Vancouver where I was part of the GB gold medal winning squad at the World Championships!

To all early years practitioners I would say - be positive, focus on the solution not the problem and most of all, let the disabled child be the one to make the choices. I am proud of the choices I made, small and large, and that has made me what I am today.

Kayleigh Black

Successful inclusive nurseries

In a successful inclusive nursery there is a positive attitude towards disabled children, where staff support and encourage children to reach their potential. In order to achieve this staff need to:

- understand the needs of children with cerebral palsy, both in terms of the condition itself and how it might affect the child's learning and development;
- review policies and practices to ensure that they do not discriminate against disabled children;
- focus on the free aspects of childhood which can be easily overlooked among all the special treatment that a disabled child might receive: play, friendship, humour, concern for others are common to all children and the child with cerebral palsy can contribute to the group in all these ways;
- address the mistaken belief that all children with cerebral palsy need one-to-one support;
- find out more about cerebral palsy and the particular needs of children with hemiplegia at these websites: www.scope.org.uk/earlyyears/ and www.hemihelp.org.uk/.

Glossary of terms

Here are some other terms you may hear when describing cerebral palsy:

- Hypertonia: too much muscle tone leading to stiffness
- Hypotonia: too little muscle tone leading to floppiness
- Dystonia: fluctuation between stiffness and floppiness
- Rigidity: sustained stiffness of a limb
- Spasm: involuntary contraction of a muscle
- Tremor: rhythmic, uncontrolled, repetitive movements
- Minimal or mild cerebral palsy: often no obvious physical impairment, but poor coordination and clumsiness, with some learning difficulties
- Monoplegia: in monoplegia only one limb (arm or leg) on one side of the body is affected; this is very rare
- Diplegia: this means that the cerebral palsy mainly affects the child's legs. Children with diplegia may also have subtle or mild muscle tone problems in the upper part of their body, but they have sufficient control for most daily activities
- Triplegia: three limbs are affected; usually one upper and two lower
- Quadriplegia: this is when cerebral palsy affects a child's whole body.

Working with parents of children with cerebral palsy

Families are on a journey with their child and the impact of the disability can follow very individual pathways. However, they will all go through similar stages. The joy of parenthood is followed by denial, anger, guilt and blame. The joy the parent feels gets mixed up with the other emotions, and how quickly parents regain that joy is to some extent tied up with the messages given out by professionals.

The extent of the disability may have little to do with where the parents are on that journey. Factors such as how they were given the news about their child's disability, how the extended family feels about them and the child and what their expectations of the child are all contribute to their state of mind. So do not assume a mild disability will have less of an impact.

Parents who are adjusting to the news that their child has a disability often need to express intense feelings. Professionals need to listen with empathy without becoming intensely sad or angry too.

The role of all professionals is to offer the family support and to accompany them on that journey. Many parents will see a lot of professionals in the early months and years of their child's life. Some will become familiar to the family but others may be seen only when needed. Families can get confused and overwhelmed by the number of professionals, the fact the professionals may use different words to describe the same things and that they don't seem to talk to each other. Encourage parents to use the parent held record books often given out by health visitors or use the Scope transition passport 'Moving Up' to capture the child's views and record progress. (Available electronically from earlyyears@scope.org.uk)

Parents may have other children, and may sometimes need advice and support in managing their family. Some young brothers and sisters will be directly involved in, and feel responsible for, the extra care needs of the disabled child. This will often lead to them having less time for themselves to enjoy their own childhood experiences. Many siblings feel invisible as their brother or sister gets much of the attention. They feel jealous of the time parents spend with the disabled brother or sister, and also feel embarrassed by their behavior in public, mostly because of how other people react. When siblings come to your setting you might be able to take an interest in them separate from their brother or sister.

Normal sibling rivalry may not be allowed in the family as parents protect the disabled child, and different standards and expectations may develop. You may be experiencing having to explain to others in the child's group that the child with cerebral palsy needs to have more time or space or why he or she cannot easily share toys. You will be working out how to explain this to the other children at the same time as trying to resolve the difficulties. The ways forward you are trying can be shared with parents and, through sharing, you may find answers together.

Sleep disturbance is often a problem, resulting in tiredness at school and extra difficulty with homework. Parents, too, may be running on very little sleep and this will add to their levels of stress.

The role of early years practitioners is to listen to the family and to support and help them as they seek solutions. You will be able to put families in touch with support networks. (See pages 81-83.)

Most importantly you will need to be honest with parents and, while making sure that every success and every step forward is the first thing that you greet them with each day, you also need to tell them when things are not going well. Try to seek possible solutions to difficulties and share these with parents. Involve parents in these solutions so that they are always aware of their importance in their child's care and education.

Enabling children to access activities

The challenge for the setting is to involve the child with cerebral palsy in the activities the other children are following throughout the day, while at the same time meeting the cerebral palsy child's own special needs. For every activity practitioners will need to ask themselves these questions:

- What are the aims for the whole group?
- What things do we do generally to include all the children in this type of activity?
- What individual adjustments will we need to make to include the child with cerebral palsy?

After the activity, practitioners will want to reflect on the way they feel it went. Ask yourself the question - how did the individual solutions I found for the child with cerebral palsy help me meet the needs of all the children? Perhaps other children were also supported? Perhaps the thinking needed helped you understand the task more completely?

For example, you might have established these aims for the group in Problem Solving, Reasoning, Numeracy:

- explore different sizes;
- recognise and name shapes;
- enjoy and join in with number songs and rhymes;
- recognise and name different colours.

The activity might go like this. The group of children sit around a table building with coloured shapes and are encouraged to discuss the colours and shapes as they play.

The child with cerebral palsy will join in these activities but may have different ways to access the materials and show what they understand:

Ben, who has difficulties in controlling his head and arms and has limited speech, will use an Etran frame to pick out colours and shapes when they are named by his supporter. Ben will sit opposite his supporter, who will be able to check easily which direction his eyes point to.

In order to achieve his outcomes, Ben will need to be supported to sit so that his feet are flat, his knees and hips are at right angles and his face and trunk are facing forward. He may be in supported seating or he may be sitting on a chair with arms. This support is necessary to allow the practitioner to sit opposite him. Other children will also need the adult's attention, so she cannot take on the physical support Ben would need to come out of his special seating.

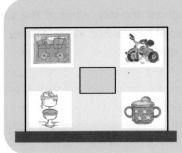

An Etran frame is a vertical Perspex oblong with a square hole in the middle and slots at the corners where the practitioner can put pictures of objects, words, letters or numbers. A child who communicates through eye pointing now has a range of options to choose from, and the practitioner can see his choice. (To see examples put 'Etran frame' in Google images.)

Jay will take part in the same task but his outcomes will be different. Jay has developmental delay as well as cerebral palsy and needs to explore these aspects of Problem Solving, Reasoning and Numeracy. Jay is sitting on a low

stool. His supporter sits behind him and supports his hips with her knees and guides his arms with her hands. She places a safely mirror in front of them so that she can check on Jay's expressions as they play together. She is also able to support the group with words and has another practitioner in the room to call on if one of the other children needs more practical support.

Jay has his own outcomes for this activity:

- **Look towards objects held in front of him.** He will be assisted to get into a good sitting position. His supporter will take time to remind him to get his feet down on the box that gives him a firm base for his feet while still being tall enough to reach the table. She has put a Dycem mat (see page 82) on his seat so that he does not slide about. She shows him a favourite toy and activates it to get his attention and then supports his right arm from behind to help him move gradually and rhythmically towards the wanted toy. She praises him. When his hands are forward he is given the toy to play with for a short time.
- The toy is put in a box out of sight and the shapes the other children are handling and building with are brought out. The shape Jay has to look at has a light attached and this flashes to get his attention.
- Jay is encouraged to **reach out and grasp the shape.** His supporter sings

a little song. 'Jay has got a square there, Jay has got a square. Jay has got a shape to hold, Jay has got a square' to the tune of 'The Sun Has Got His Hat On'.

- Show awareness of familiar songs through animated facial expressions. Jay smiles when the song is sung and moves the shape up and down.
- Look at a coloured square against contrasting background. His supporter places the brightly coloured square, without a flashing light, on a dark contrasting background and holds it up in front of Jay's eyes. She moves it slowly to the right and then to the left. She notes that he follows easily to the right but that he loses the shape as it moves a few centimetres to the left. She will start with the left tomorrow as it might be that he is tired.

When the activity is finished the practitioner praises Jay for his efforts.

Jay now needs to transfer into his supported seat for snack time. The practitioner working with Jay asks the other person in the room to position his chair close by. Jay is able to weight bear, and this is an important aspect of his learning.

- The practitioner has been taught by his therapist to help him grasp the edge of the table and push through his hips and knees into a supported standing position.
- She tells Jay to put his hands on the table.
- She supports him at his hips to push down through his legs and lift his bottom.
- The other practitioner pulls the stool away and replaces it with the supportive seat.
- The practitioner sings a little song to remind Jay that he is standing, 'Jay is standing tall, Jay is standing tall, 1,2,3,4,5 Jay is standing tall' to the tune of 'The Farmer's in his Den'.
- She tells Jay he is going to sit down
- She counts Jay down into sitting
        - 'I bend my knees 1,2,3'
        - 'I ... sit ... down' (slowly giving emphasis on each word).

For some children with cerebral palsy talking is very difficult. For these children the setting will need to have a variety of strategies in place to help them to access activities.

Julie has cerebral palsy affecting all four limbs. She is very sociable and gets frustrated at not being able to communicate. The setting has worked hard to overcome this.

During story time Julie has her own story sack and the objects representing the story are put on the tray of her chair. Julie can play with these as she listens to the story. When questions are asked the practitioner tells Julie she will need to answer a question:

- 'Julie, in a minute I want you to tell me who was naughty in the story.'
- Julie's supporter offers Julie a choice of two, a girl doll and a toy puppy.
- Julie waves her arm toward the puppy. Her supporter gives her the toy to hold and puts the others away.
- When the story teller sees that Julie has chosen her answer she comes back to Julie saying, 'Julie, can you show everyone which one in the story was naughty?'
- Julie waves the puppy and it falls out of her grip.
- The story teller laughs and says, 'Yes, it was a very naughty PUPPY and it's still being naughty. It is trying to run away!'
- If Julie had chosen a different answer, such as the girl doll, the story teller could have asked the group if they agreed with Julie that perhaps the little girl in the story was naughty sometimes.

Connor also has cerebral palsy that affects all his limbs, and his hands are tightly clenched. At the start of every session his supporter uses a warm water hand bath and then gently strokes the back of his hand to relax it. Once relaxed, Connor can extend a finger to point and with this he can communicate.

Connor has a Go Talk 4+ communicator (see page 83) and he loves to chat. He has four pictures to press and each one carries a short message. The talker can store 16 messages giving four different possible conversations, and always shows 'yes' and 'no' for answering questions. Today the group are talking about going to the park. The practitioner has stuck pictures of a roundabout, a slide, a swing and an ice cream to the card in the little machine, and recorded a short phrase for each. The children are talking about what they want to do. Connor keeps touching a picture on his talker and a voice rings out 'I want ice cream.'

His supporter laughs and tells him that everyone will get an ice cream, and asks again what ride he wants to go on. This time he presses the picture of a roundabout. The voice rings out, 'I want to ride the roundabout'. He is told that he will ride on the roundabout, and they set off.

When they get back from the park the children are going to draw a picture of their trip. Connor is given a number of pictures of garden play equipment cut out from a catalogue. He chooses which ones he wants to use and his supporter helps him extend a finger so that he can spread paste over the paper, and he also helps press each picture down.

Freddie needs to come out of his supportive seating and spend time on the floor. It is very important that he uses this time to best advantage so his supporter helps him to solve the problem of changing from sitting to lying. The room has a carpeted corner and Freddie can lie over some rolled up blankets, which support his chest.

- Freddie's supporter helps him take some weight through his feet and legs as he moves from the chair to the floor.
- His feet, then his knees, then his hips, side and shoulder touch the carpet in turn. This gives him messages about changing position.
- He lies on his side then rolls on to his back.
- His supporter encourages him to raise his left hand above his head and helps him bring his right knee up and across his body.
- She says 'I ... roll ... over', giving slow emphasis to each word.
- She assists him to follow his knee and roll over on to his tummy.
- She asks him to bring both hands forward and reach out in front of him.
- She helps him bring his hands back to prop on his elbows.
- She puts the rolled-up blankets under his chest.
- His hands are now free to play with toy cars which he particularly likes.

Developing skills to initiate activities

All children will need to develop listening and attention skills and the child with cerebral palsy will also need to develop skills in pointing with finger or eyes in order to be able to take the lead in play and activities.

Levels of attention

- Attention to sights and sounds. For some children with cerebral palsy this stage can last a long time. If this is the case give the child lots of sensory stimulation.
- The child shows good attention to a task of his own choosing and cannot easily be distracted.

At this stage the child will have very few activities or items that capture their attention. Try to extend the range of activities the child will accept. For example if he likes the toy telephone try to extend the types of phone he will play with, or engage with him in a pretend conversation.

- Pays attention to a task of the adult's choosing if the adult shares this with him. Many of the younger children will be at this stage of attention. You will want to extend the time the child with cerebral palsy can spend enjoying the book or toy while you are with another child. You may stay with her but withdraw your full attention to encourage another child, or you may continue to talk to the child with cerebral palsy as you physically move away from her.
- Maintains attention to the activity chosen for a limited time but finds difficulty in returning to the activity if distracted. Notice how long the child stays enjoying the activity and offer praise. Keep a record of his attention and reward with stars or smiley faces. Notice his attention. 'Jack. What a good boy you are playing so well with your cars.' A comment like this not only lets Jack know that you are still interested but specifically mentions the behaviour you are trying to encourage and can redirect him back to that activity. Children need to be at this level of attention before more structured work can be expected. This could be building blocks, jigsaw or colouring in that the child is expected to complete independently.

- **Switches attention between the activity and other interesting things th** goes back to the activity. Children at this level can look up from a task, see what is gong on and then get back in task without an adult needing to remind them.

Pointing

You don't need hands to use pointing as a means of communication. Children who will never use their hands effectively can become excellent communicators. In this area this can mean extending a finger to point but  some children will use another part of the body to point. There is a range of head pointers available, or the child may use feet, knees, shoulders and elbows to point and access a switch to operate a toy or communication aid. The speech and language therapist will advise on the best use of communication aids and the setting can also produce a communication passport for the child telling everyone how the child communicates and what her like and dislikes are.

Children want to play and through careful observation you will discover how the child with cerebral palsy lets you know what he wants to play with:

- The child may cry to get attention, and that often results in the adult supporter offering a choice of items until the child is satisfied. This is exhausting for the child, the supporter and everyone else, so it is important to find a more appropriate and effective way to respond.
- First find out what the child really likes. Whatever this is, place it on a flat tray in front of the child. Draw attention to it and watch what she does.
- The child may try to move his arm or fist towards the item. Once you notice this movement give the child the item or activate the toy.
- Once the child realises that he will get the toy if he makes this effort he will be more motivated and you can extend the activity to touching the toy. In the beginning he may need adult help, but expect that he will do more and more himself.
- Once she is able to touch the item, move it around on the tray or table.
- Discover how far she can reach. Ideally you would like her to reach into four corners of the tray. However, if she cannot manage that you will know where to place items so that she CAN reach them.

Another way for the child to initiate an activity is to look towards it. This is known as 'Eye Pointing'. Just like pointing with a fist or finger it is very useful to the child and can be extended into a formal method of communicating and requesting toys or activities.

Activities to promote eye pointing

For every activity you will need to think about a reward that is really motivating. It may be food or a sound-making toy. Once you have decided what you are going to offer the child you need to gain their attention!

- Sit facing the child. Look at her. Say her name then, 'Look at me'.
- As you speak you may need to get near or gently touch her face, then draw your finger back towards your own eyes
- With some children you may have to use a noisy or light-reflecting toy to get attention.
- Hold the toy at eye level and watch to see if the child looks towards it.

Once you know she can look at a toy or item you can slowly move it around and see if she can follow it with her eyes. Just like finger pointing, looking to four corners is the ideal but wherever you find she can look you will know where to position items for her to choose from.

Scope has an activity pack to promote eye pointing, and the Call Centre has a simple downloadable guide to using Etran frames and eye pointing. http://callcentre.education.ed.ac.uk/downloads/quickguides/aac/etran.pdf

Self Help

Children with cerebral palsy will want to be as independent as possible in the areas of dressing and undressing, toileting, eating and drinking. Each individual will face different challenges in these areas, and practitioners should

seek advice from the child's parents and the professionals offering support. The occupational therapist will be able to give particular help in these areas.

Many children with cerebral palsy find sitting difficult and will need several different types of seat to access all areas of self help. Most will need to be able to take up a range of positions using supported and less supported seating throughout the day.

Unless told otherwise, most children will get the best support from sitting with feet flat, bottom back and knees and hips as close to right angles as the child can manage. This could be achieved through a specially designed chair but a sturdy chair with a back and sides, or a sturdy stool, can sometimes be used instead. Floor corner seats are also useful to ensure the child has a chance to experience floor play, and can be a good place to start undressing skills.

Unless directed by the child's therapist, it is not usually wise for the child to spend time in lie-back baby chairs or on bean bags. Baby walkers may give the impression of freedom but they usually encourage all the wrong types of movement and can lead to real difficulties later on.

Children using the floor to sit, lie or prop should have enough space and may need extra room to roll or into a sitting position. Kneeling up to play at a low table can be useful, but they should be discouraged from leaning back so that they sit between their knees.

Children need to practise the movements for dressing and undressing every day. These can form part of the music and movement activities the group enjoys. Lying on the floor and grasping in both hands a brightly painted dowel rod that has bells or ribbons on each end can help the child move up from the chest position to extending the 'barbell' backwards over his head. This stretch is very good for all his muscles and prepares him for helping to extend his arm to put on his coat or jumper. You could sing 'The Grand old Duke of York' and the stretch could be the top of the hill. The activity to make the barbells could involve the whole group and the singing and stretching will be fun and good for all children.

Undressing is easier than dressing. Ask the family to dress the child in loose clothes and, where possible, to replace buttons and zips with Velcro fastenings and elasticated waistbands. Cotton clothes are easier to take off than synthetic materials.

Talk to the child's parents about how they encourage her to help with undressing. Pulling off shoes and socks is a good place to start.

- Help the child to achieve a good sitting position on the mat. If this is difficult, a small rolled-up towel under the back of the hips can provide a wedge to stabilise sitting. If the child cannot achieve sitting this can be done in a lying position.

- Help the child to get one leg bent at the knee with that foot flat on the floor (or as best as he can manage).
- Help the child bring that foot to rest on the extended leg at or around the knee joint.
- Wait for the child to be able to look at this foot.
- Guide the child's hand down to the shoe and assist her to push it off (loosen tight buckles or laces first).
- Work the sock three quarters off the child's foot then help her to get a hand to the sock to grasp it and pull it off.
- Repeat for the other foot.

NOW do something exciting to reward the child for the effort. For example, he could paddle in water or sand OR JELLY!

Taking off a cardigan can be another place to start. Cardigans are much easier than jumpers! In everyday play you will be asking the child to extend his arm outwards to play with toys and above his head for action songs. This is important practice for dressing and undressing.

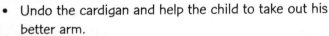
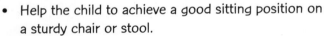

- Help the child to achieve a good sitting position on a sturdy chair or stool.
- Undo the cardigan and help the child to take out his better arm.
- Give the child time to get his balance and bring his head and hands forward so that they are facing front.
- The child needs to be able to look at his hands.
- Pull the cuff a little way beyond his hand.
- Help the child to keep the arm in the cardigan sleeve in sight and encourage him to grab his cuff.
- You may need to give him a little extra support at his shoulders or hips so that he can feel safe enough to tug on the cuff.
- Encourage him to keep pulling and give a little help if needed.
- Celebrate hugely once this is done!

Taking off trousers or a skirt is really difficult. For trousers follow the suggestions for socks and shoes having removed the more difficult leg first. Skirts are easiest to remove when standing.

- Help the child to a safe standing position as shown by the parents or therapist. This is often standing, supported by hands grasping a table at the right height.

- Sit on a low stool or the floor behind the child ready to give extra support if needed.
- Move the skirt to just below the hips and encourage the child to move on the spot causing the skirt to fall. You may need to give extra support at the hips for her to feel safe in this activity.
- This is a good opportunity to practise stepping so help her to raise one foot, then the other and disentangle the skirt.

Even very small children can learn to cooperate in dressing and undressing. Children who still need nappies or pads can learn to lift their bottoms to help.

- Lying on his back the child is helped to bring up his knees and place his feet flat as close to his bottom as he can manage.
- The practitioner holds his feet in that position and encourages him to lift his bottom off the floor.
- If the child tries the supporter gives him huge praise and tries to get the child's favourite toy 'under the bridge'.
- Two or three tries a day are enough.
- This bridge activity can also be used to help slide shorts or trousers up when dressing.

Eating and drinking

Children with cerebral palsy are very likely to need to learn extra skills to help them to eat and drink. For some children swallowing is difficult or deemed unwise, so they are given meals through a tube that either goes into the stomach directly or is passed through their nose into the stomach. For a very few children the tube passes through the stomach into the jejunum. This type of tube is called a 'J tube'. These children have

> Many children with cerebral palsy find it difficult to eat and drink enough to stay well and grow, and around 60% will actually need more food than classmates of a similar age because tense muscles and constant muscle movement require more energy. They need frequent, high calorie snacks and drinks to take in enough nourishment.

continuous feeds passed directly into the jejunum just below the stomach throughout the day and night. Staff must be trained by a qualified person before dealing with a child who is tube fed. The Local Authority will provide guidance on who is the proper person to give this training. It could be the health visitor or a specialist children's nurse.

More commonly children with cerebral palsy will have difficulty with the mechanics of chewing and swallowing and will need to have their food prepared to a particular consistency. Some children are extremely fussy eaters and tolerate only a very limited range of foods. For some this is because early choking and reflux (an extreme form of heartburn) made eating so unpleasant that they are anxious about trying anything new. Others may have had limited contact with food because of early swallowing difficulties and tube feeding, which means they are starting at the baby stage of tasting solids at three or four years old.

Whatever the reasons, eating and drinking difficulties need to be considered in the sessions the child spends away from the family. A risk assessment should be undertaken, including the family and relevant professionals such as the speech and language therapist or the children's nurse. If there is thought to be a risk staff should ask for training to ensure safety. However if the problem is about tempting the child to try different foods there might not be a need for training, just perseverance and devising ways to make the food attractive and unthreatening.

There are many utensils on the market to assist the child to get food on to a spoon or fork and take it to the mouth. A good sitting position is essential, and time to chew and swallow more slowly. Warm food may go cold, so it may be necessary to heat only a small amount at a time. Some children will come into the setting using a bottle and the move to a feeder cup or a sloped 'Doidy cup' should be discussed with parents. The Doidy cup allows a very small amount of liquid to be drunk at a time and does not require the arms to lift high. (See pages 81-83 for suppliers.)

While the right equipment, time and patience all support the child with cerebral palsy to learn the skills of eating and drinking, the most motivating factor will be play. Food play and tasting sessions, smelly food experiments and food squelching will help many children overcome their anxiety about food. (Scope has published *Food Talks*, a guide for parents and carers on some of the difficulties around eating and drinking. See page 83 for details.)

Self help and personal care

Whether the child needs full personal care from an adult or reminders to visit the toilet she will need to gain as much independence as possible. Regular visits to the toilet area throughout the day give the child many opportunities to practise standing, weight bearing and sitting in less supported seats. Sitting on a potty is a good way to start, as the child can sit and look at a wipe clean book or play with a washable toy.

Specialist toilet aids cost a great deal but there are several simple seat type potties available from high street shops. When the child is ready to move from just sitting to 'performing' you could put a crinkled sheet of foil in the bottom of the potty so that any action is noticed and praised at the right time. It is possible to buy potties that play a tune when wet. The Fisher Price Royal Potty has the back and sides to support a small child with cerebral palsy and can be found in high street stores and on the internet at www.fisher-price.com/uk/

Children with cerebral palsy, like any other children, need to be reminded of why they need to wash their hands and this is also another opportunity to stand and bear weight, reach, and grasp and release the soap and flannel.

You will need to work together with parents and other settings the child attends, to provide a consistent approach to toilet routines. Children with cerebral palsy may need the safety of the potty for longer than others in their group and these, with others who are receiving full personal care, will need a safe and private place to receive the support they need. Creating this space may involve using screens or a curtain to achieve a degree of privacy or using the staff toilet if there is sufficient space.

Encourage the child to pay attention to the hygiene routine after using the toilet or being changed.

Multi-agency work

Who's who?

The Children Act (2006) sees multi-agency working as key to ensuring that we meet the outcomes for *Every Child Matters*.

The child with cerebral palsy will usually have contact with a range of professionals who support them and their family. They provide information and guidance, ans some may be able to help obtain vital equipment.

Educational psychologist (EP)

Assesses the child's development and provides support and advice on learning and behaviour. The family will probably already have contact but you still need to talk to them first before you make an approach. They work for the local authority and respond to requests from all agencies and families. Your Area SENCo can put you in touch.

Health visitor and specialist health visitor (HV)

Can help with practical advice and support on day-to-day matters such as feeding or sleeping. In some local authorities there are specialist health visitors who are designated to train staff on, for example, tube feeding or administering Epi-pens (for severe reactions to allergies) or other medication. Ask your Area SENCo if there are Specialist HVs who can help you.

Specialist pre-school teaching support and Portage

Many local authorities have pre-school teaching and home visiting services. Ask your Area SENCo what the service is called in your area and what support they might be able to provide to children in your setting.

Portage is a home-visiting educational service for pre-school children with additional support needs and their families, also sometimes used in schools and nurseries. Portage Home Visitors are very helpful in showing early years settings what the child can do and how to support the child to do it. They will often make an initial visit to the setting with the parents and may assist the transition into early years education and daycare.

Physiotherapist

Physiotherapy is the treatment of disorders of movement and function caused by problems in the muscles, bones or nervous system. Physiotherapists assess and work with children. They also advise parents and carers on how to lift and position their child safely and properly. They may teach parents a series of exercises that can be used regularly to help the child at home and in the setting.

Occupational therapist

May work with parents to develop physical or learning skills, using special play equipment. Can also advise on equipment to help mobility, like tricycles and trolleys. Sometimes gives advice about equipment and aids to help the child with everyday activities, like eating.

Speech and language therapist (SALT)

Some children with cerebral palsy have delayed language because they're not able to play and explore the world in the same way as other children. A SALT can work with practitioners and families to plan suitable learning activities. May also help with alternative communication systems (sign language, symbols or communication aids and devices) for children who have major language or speech problems. May meet parents very early on if the child has problems with feeding, drinking or swallowing.

There are many other professionals who may be involved including:

Teachers of children with visual and hearing impairment

Clinical psychologists

Community paediatricians

Social services workers

Specialist play workers

Staff in child development centres and hospitals

Co-ordinators of opportunity groups and parent partnerships.

See the case study of Alice on the next page for an example of agencies working together.

Great ideas for working together

Parents generally take their child to a clinic or specialist setting to get therapy support and you will need to set some time aside to learn from parents after these visits. There may be times when you could free up the child's Key Person to go along to a session and learn directly from the therapist.

Therapists trust parents to pass on their knowledge and skill, and in most cases they can show practitioners the simple exercises that will help. However if the needs of the child are very complex, ask for training direct from the therapists.

It is often helpful if the therapist writes down some ideas for you to try to save the parents from an additional worry of how they are going to pass on information to you.

There are many other ways you can support the child. You may have a child like Alice in your group. At three years old Alice is not yet walking, crawling or saying more than a few words. You are not sure she sees everything clearly and her hands cannot easily hold paintbrushes and crayons. Mum is a single parent and has another, older child who goes to a school 30 minutes walk away.

> Your Area SENCo will know which procedures, such as tube feeding or administering medication, require training and who is responsible for providing it.

Somehow many different professionals must find ways of working together to become an efficient team for the child. The first step is to set up an appointments diary with mum so that you know when she is seeing each of the professionals. Keep it up to date so you don't miss an opportunity to give and receive information. Keep your own diary of Alice's progress and your questions and concerns. Go through both diaries with mum regularly and give her the information in writing to take to each appointment. This should be clear and simple and should always start with all the positive things the child is doing.

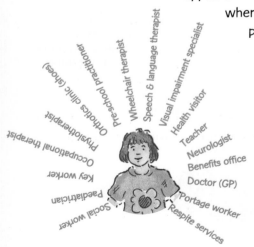

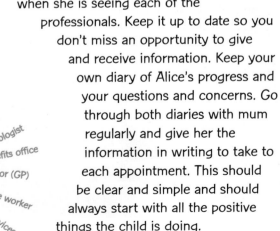

The visual impairment specialist will be very interested in how you think Alice is using her vision in the group. You could record how long she pays attention to items or people, whether she pays more attention to bright, shiny or colourful things, whether she brings everything near to her face or likes to watch the movement of trees and birds out of the window. You will want to ask the visual impairment specialist teacher if there are ways in which you can make toys and books more accessible to Alice.

The educational psychologist (EP) will be helping Alice's mum think about the next stage of schooling. They will want to know how much she benefits from being part of the early years setting and what specialist support she needs. It is important when you are reporting to the EP that you list all the positive things about inclusion first. The difficulties are obvious but the benefits of friendship and being part of a language rich setting are sometimes overlooked in our rush to provide for all the special needs.

For example you might know just how much Alice enjoys sand and water play with the other children. You can tell the psychologist how sociable she is and how she offers toys to the other children and smiles. You can also tell him that if she had equipment to help her stand by the trays she would actually be able to play with her friends independently. This means that her abilities in independent play are restricted more by the lack of equipment than her own impairments.

> ### Helping Hands Nursery
>
> Name: Alice Young   Date: 24/10/2008
>
> Alice comes to nursery on Tuesday and Wednesday each week. Her mother has told us she is visiting the Speech and Language Therapist this week and we thought we would let you know how she is getting on. Alice is using a lot of different sounds and facial expressions and generally lets us know what she likes and doesnt like. She clearly loves to press the switch to make the remote control car whizz about.
>
> She is very sociable and likes to play in the company of other children. She is just as good as the others at taking turns. She loves story sack time and handles the appropriate toys as we read about them.
>
> We would like to help Alice communicate with the other children better. If you have any ideas of how we could help Alice communicate more easily we would be happy to try them out.
>
> Looking forward to hearing from you.
>
> Jane Bankes (Key Worker)

This sort of information can be used to ensure smooth transition to school.

Dual placements: working together with families and other settings

The EYFS framework emphasises the need for all settings to make sure they understand the number of different carers a child may have and states clearly that effective communication between settings is key to ensuring that children's needs are met and that there is continuity in their learning.

When we are weaning a child off the bottle or dummy or trying to establish a toilet routine the differences in these settings may make the task more difficult, so it is important to work together to achieve some consistency. Your setting may need to take the lead in bringing this about.

Nathan is three and is still dependent on his dummy. He gets anxious when he cannot have it. The setting he attends is keen to eliminate the dummy and therefore needs strong communication links with parents and other carers to achieve this.

Step 1: Nathan's Key Person talks to his parents about using the dummy at home. He usually only has the dummy at night but if other children come to the house he gets anxious and parents often give him his dummy as a comforter. He also uses the dummy when he goes to his grandparents.

Step 2: Parents and Key Person agree to observe Nathan for a week in different settings and see what the triggers for his anxiety are. They ask themselves whether it might be the movement of other children, the additional noise, or the uncertainty about what might happen next.

Step 3: They meet and discuss their findings
- At home Nathan becomes anxious if there are noisy children in the house.
- At his grandparents' he becomes anxious when the children come home from school and play in the garden next door.
- In the setting they cannot be so sure that noise is the trigger and think other children moving near him may play a part as well.

Step 4: They talk about possible ways forward. Nathan likes music. They decide to make a cosy corner with cushions and the music system. To learn that he can go there, he will be shown how to go and switch on music when he is not anxious. When he becomes anxious, rather than give him his dummy, an adult will take him to the cosy corner and help him put on music, staying with him until he is calm.

They agree to meet again and discuss how well this is working. Other ways to work together could involve setting up a diary system.

Daisy, aged 20 months, attends a mainstream group and a School for Parents. Her mainstream setting would like Daisy to sit independently. It would help her participate in play. Her mother asks the specialist group if they can teach her this skill. Mum explains to staff that, in the specialist group, Daisy is helped to sit with her legs flexed and ankles crossed with a towel rolled and placed under her spine to help her balance. Her arms are helped to come forward with hands on the floor between her legs. Mum is excited because Daisy has held this position for a few seconds before toppling to one side.

Mainstream staff are keen to help Daisy but are worried she might hurt herself or be knocked over by other children. They ask mum to take some photographs. When they see the photos they see that Daisy is sitting surrounded by cushions. The next snap captures her laughing face as she topples on to the cushions and then her determined face as she is helped to try again. Seeing how it is achieved in the specialist setting gives the staff confidence to try. A few weeks later she is trying this every day at home and in both her placements. Daisy achieves a ten second sit and gets a certificate.

Daisy has benefited from the willingness of each service to learn from the other and from having different settings to develop her new skill. The special setting has listened to the needs of the mainstream setting and the mainstream setting has arranged the environment to produce a safe place for Daisy to practise.

Mainstream staff can spend time with Daisy in the specialist setting and learn a lot of new skills. Specialist staff can write a drinking programme for Daisy to follow at home and in mainstream. Mainstream can let the specialist setting know how vocal Daisy has become as she plays alongside others in the home corner.

Daisy's parents feel that she gets the best of both worlds: she has a specialist team working on the tiny steps needed to support her in learning new skills and the mainstream setting is supporting her in using them in a noisier and busier environment. This dual placement is giving Daisy the best possible chance of making the greatest progress.

The child with cerebral palsy may need to visit one or more services to meet a variety of needs. These may be formal or informal Dual Placements for their children. Families make these arrangements because they think they will get the child's full range of needs met.

Benefits of Dual Placements

Many children with cerebral palsy will need to have therapies such as physiotherapy, speech and language therapy, occupational therapy or music therapy. They may attend:

~ Opportunities Group;
~ special playgroup;
~ special needs school nursery;
~ hospital or clinic based therapies;
~ Bobath therapy;
~ School for Parents (a specialist group where parents learn how to support their child's learning and physical needs).

Some families may value meeting other families where children have cerebral palsy so that they can benefit from sharing their experiences.

When we talk to parents about their child's experiences at these groups we need to think about what the child can generalise into our setting and how we can help this to happen.

Inclusive practice - what does it look like?

Good inclusive practice is confident in giving all parents the warm welcome they want for their children. Confidence comes from staff who are trained and supported in making the adjustments needed for the child with cerebral palsy as part of the everyday planning they do for all children.

Ethos and attitudes, the way we think about disabled children

The ethos and attitude evident in the setting shows an underlying commitment. Good practice ensures that all policies are inclusive and the ethos and methods followed in the setting should be evident through all aspects of its practice. However, settings will need to have a formal inclusion policy to make their attitudes and approaches clear to all.

Family/parent involvement

Effective inclusive settings value the family and remember how much they may be able to help practitioners while at the same time ensuring that the setting supports them. Systems are put into place to ensure information is shared between

No child exists in isolation. Even families who seem to be well informed and understanding of their child's disability will have been on a journey, often of pain and frustration.

families and the setting. Ensure each child has a home/nursery notebook. Practitioners can write what the child has done that day and this will facilitate family/child discussion. This book can also be used for passing on any daily information or asking questions.

Physical environment

Effective inclusive practice considers how the building appears to a child with cerebral palsy. Some children with cerebral palsy will be walking well, some will walk with difficulty or with an aid such as crutches or a rollator (a

wheeled walking aid), some will use a manual wheelchair that they propel themselves and some will use an electric wheelchair.

Practitioners will recognise that some children will have additional difficulties that may make the building less easy to access. Some will have hearing loss and others may have hypersensitive hearing. Some may have low vision and others may be acutely sensitive to glare. Some children may have difficulty dealing with the movement of large numbers of other children around them. Some may fall frequently or have difficulty getting back up when they fall. The good inclusive service considers all these aspects and puts training and support for staff in place. Staff walk around the building. They ask, are cupboards, coat racks, coats, bags, etc., cluttering up the spaces? Are any floor-tiles loose or damaged? Do doors open fully? What risks can practitioners see with regard to glass in doors or for displays?

Settings will want to look at their general disability access and how, within affordability, access might be improved. Access is about more than just the ways into and around the building. It is about the way the setting thinks about the colours used on walls and boards, and whether this is good for visual communication. It is also about the way the setting thinks about the noise levels and how to reduce them for children with sensitive hearing or hearing impairments. Settings will also want to think about the way light enters the rooms and whether glare could be a problem for some children.

Session/activity planning

The EYFS framework places an expectation for differentiation for all children with additional needs, not just those with statements or identified disabilities. It is this range of differentiation that marks good inclusive practice. For example, session planning for story time may involve supporting the pictures in the book with symbols. This helps children using symbols to communicate. However, if the story was also supported with a bag of real/tactile objects it would also help children with learning difficulties and those with visual impairment.

Activities provided by other people

When other people come into the setting to offer activities it is important to plan for these to be effective.

For example, a visiting puppet show that lasts 20 minutes and involves strobe lighting is not inclusive for the child who has a five minute attention span and is hypersensitive to light. Effective inclusive practice puts time into preparation beforehand with the organisers to remove the strobe lighting from the first five minutes and ensure a complete five minute section at the start. This could give the child a really positive experience.

Preparation for changing settings

Anxiety and excitement are the common feelings around transition, from an early education setting/class to Reception/Key Stage1, and between key stages in a school. There will most likely be different staff, rooms, buildings and a new more formal curriculum.

Children with cerebral palsy are at risk every time there is a big change, as they may have fewer resources to make adaptations and may rely far more heavily on the receiving school to make these adaptations on their behalf.

Good inclusive practice thinks ahead, considering wider issues than just the educational implications. It considers and plans for the predicable changes moving to Reception/Key Stage 1 will bring (changes in the height and weight of the child, in the amount and type of class work expected, and the social needs of the next stage) and tries to predict those not at first expected.

Health and safety regulations

The publication *The Dignity of Risk* compiled by the Council for Disabled Children gives clear health and safety guidance.

Good inclusive practice understands the need for risk. Risk is a learning tool. If children are never allowed to take risks they never mature into adults who can take control of their own lives. Healthy risk taking has to be at the heart of all the educational experiences practitioners give children: the risk of failure, the risk of sadness, the risk of friendship, the risk of knowledge. Without risk learning does not advance.

> All settings need to be familiar with the regulations and guidance on managing risk, manual handling, children's healthcare and physical interventions and how to apply them and where to get support and guidance.

Good inclusive settings place the child at the heart of all their planning and processes and accept difference as a learning curve that will enhance the education and care they give to all children.

Children with cerebral palsy and the EYFS curriculum

The new EYFS framework offers the opportunity to adapt and meet needs at all developmental levels, making it an excellent starting point to include children with cerebral palsy in early years settings. Children with cerebral palsy will have a wide range of difficulties relating to how they physically access activities and how they learn from them. This section of the book looks at the ways we can include children with cerebral palsy in each of the six learning and development areas of the EYFS.

Personal Social and Emotional Development

Every child with cerebral palsy is different and will have different physical and learning needs requiring different types and levels of support. In order to develop their dispositions and attitudes each child will need:

- the opportunity to influence the world around them;
- to be heard. Listen and respond to their communication, whether it is crying, attempting words or body language it will reassure the child they are known and can express preferences;
- to be offered real choices, for example in activities, snacks or friendship groups. Respect the child's choice, even if you think it is a mistake. This way the child learns that choices have consequences.

The child will develop self confidence and self esteem through earning praise and recognition.

- If the children are playing 'going to the vet', one way to ensure that the child has the same opportunities to play the most important role is to make the child with cerebral palsy the vet with a white coat, stethoscope and thermometer.
- If the child has limited communication and mobility other children will automatically find ways to include him in the play and the child will learn that they are necessary and important within their peer group.

It is vital that the child makes good relationships with family, staff, volunteers and the children in the group and not just with a personal supporter:

> Dan loves racing cars so the staff used painted card to turn the push-along trolley car into a formula one racer. Dan put on the red tabard and helmet and sat in the driver's seat. Other boys piled in and began to 'vroom-vroom' around the room.

- Use the child's communication method with all the staff and children.
- If the child uses pictures, symbols, signing or objects to support communication they need to be part of the day for all the children and staff.
- Use the communication methods to encourage all children to share and take turns.
- Use 'Command games' to promote a shared activity (see the display box on the next page).

Research shows that children with cerebral palsy have a greater possibility of a behaviour difficulty directly associated with cerebral palsy. It will take longer for many of them to establish appropriate behaviour and self control.

Command game
(giving adults silly things to do)

1. The child chooses an adult (eye or finger pointing).
2. The child then indicates one of the pictures.
3. The adult confirms the picture choice by pointing to it and saying, 'You have chosen the KANGAROO - you want me to hop like a KANGAROO'.
4. The child indicates if the choice is correct.
5. The adult performs the action enthusiastically!
6. The child chooses another adult and repeats.
(Other children in the group can join in the game and will have fun performing the actions.)

- Adapt the environment to create a calm oasis where the child can choose to retreat from the demands of the group and be supported to overcome fears and anxieties.
- The oasis can be used to teach alternative responses to anxiety and learn calming techniques like counting in and out of activities or using the traffic light system where red, orange and green coloured discs are used to support changing activities. Teach the system through the traffic lights game (see below).

Tommy has mild cerebral palsy, learning difficulties and autism. From time to time he finds the group too much to deal with.
After discussions with his parents the room is rearranged to provide a tented corner where he can choose to retreat with a favourite toy. He is allowed a set time within the tent then encouraged out to try again. However on bad days he may spend a considerable time in the tent, so the supporter brings another child to play with toys alongside him.

Traffic lights

Make three 'traffic lights' from lollypop sticks and circles of green, orange and red card. Green for 'go', orange for 'get ready' and red for 'stop'. Start with green and red and only introduce orange when the game is learnt.

Play a tune or sing a song, getting the child to signal start (green) and stop (red). Obey the signals but once the game is familiar make a few mistakes and let the child correct you.

As the child gets confident introduce more actions (running, standing, sitting, etc.). Introduce the orange stick getting her to cue in starting and stopping.

You can play this with groups of children, taking turns to hold the sticks.

- Use these techniques with all the children.
- Teach everyone caring attitudes with plenty of opportunities to practise them.
- Use emoticons or pictures to support understanding of emotions. This gives all the children another emotional voice that does not rely on speech or vocabulary, to express how they are feeling.
- Make time every day to discuss feelings and express moods.

Self care is an area most children with cerebral palsy will have greatest difficulty with.

- Start by giving choices of what apron to wear for water play, what clothes to try on when dressing up and so on.
- The child can then move to being cooperative when being dressed and undressed and can learn reaching and stretching movements to support dressing.
- If the child can sit independently a secure stool can be used to give the child more access to their feet. Dressing can be started by an adult but completed by the child.
- Children with cerebral palsy may wobble when reaching and stretching. This is part of their problem-solving. This means that while they may need to be in a supportive seat for some activities they also need to be in less supported seats for other activities. Reaching requires the child to move the head, shoulders and arm, not just the arm alone, and this may look wobbly.

> Mandy is very keen to help with dressing and undressing. Her parents have sent in looser cotton socks with wide tops. Her supporter helps her sit on the low stool and bring one ankle to rest on her other knee. Mandy needs to start with pulling her socks off. Her supporter pulls the sock a little way off her toes then rolls the sock down to the end of her foot. Mandy reaches to her foot and grasps her sock pulling it off and achieving success.

- Sit behind the child with your knees either side of the child so you can close them up to give more support if needed and can also reach forward to guide arms.
- In hygiene routines the child can rub hands together for washing and can practise spitting in tooth cleaning routines.
- Make sure there is enough time for the child to practise these independent parts of self care and celebrate and record each little bit they can do.

- Give instructions to the rest of the group in plenty of time for the child with cerebral palsy to change position or activity. The child with cerebral palsy will need extra time to finish the activity or change from the floor to a chair or from the table to a sit and ride toy. This will enable the child with cerebral palsy to be a real part of the group.

Many children with cerebral palsy are isolated by the good intentions of the adults who support them. In order to develop a sense of community the child needs to take part in group play and other group activities:

- When the group is raising money for charity with a sponsored toddle round the park the child can join in with their walker or chair and might be sponsored for the independent movements they make.
- When planning community visits use story sack techniques to introduce the child to the idea.
- Check accessibility and make sure that everyone has the knowledge and skill to communicate directly with the child. Take some items of the child's communication such as appropriate pictures or objects to show the group, that the child will be familiar with, that can be used while the group of children are being given information.
- If the visit involves eating or drinking think how the child with cp can be included. For some children a tiny taste smeared just inside the bottom lip is enough. Check this with the child's parents.

Communication, Language and Literacy

Most children with cerebral palsy that affects all four limbs will have problems affecting speech, and some will also have problems affecting the way they process communication in the brain. Children with hemiplegia and diplegia may have clear speech and some good expressive social language but can also have the same language processing difficulties particularly when answering a direct question or trying to remember.

Some children with cerebral palsy will have very good spoken communication - usually those with hemiplegia and diplegia where the muscle groups for controlling the face are not affected.

The child will need to use language for communication. If he has good speech it is still important to monitor their development of the understanding and use of language. Where the child does not have clear speech there must be other ways to develop an effective communication system.

There are many different ways to support communication:

- Signing systems such as Makaton and Signalong are often used in the early years although children with cerebral palsy who are also deaf may be learning British Sign Language from the beginning.
- Picture and symbol communication systems are most useful for children with poor use of their hands. These children can point or look towards a picture or symbol.
- Some of the youngest children may be learning to relate activities to objects.
- For all of these the child should be receiving the support of a speech and language therapist who will be able to offer advice.

Now you have an idea of how the child understands you will be able to improve the child's use of language for thinking. You have to make sure that the language you use to him is appropriate and at the right developmental level and that you are giving lots of opportunities NOT just for him to respond to questions but also for him to:

- initiate conversations;
- tell you things he likes to do.

If the child needs to use pictures or symbols to do this you could download the free materials to support using Augmentative and Alternative Communication (AAC) from the scope website (see page 82).

Many children with cerebral palsy have great difficulty linking sounds and letters as they do not have good use of muscles of the tongue, throat and lips needed to make the sounds happen.

These children need to follow a visual approach to rhyming words so that they can link them in this way. Lots of pantomime such as:

The ball had a fall - acted out

The dog fell off a log - using toys or puppets.

> Sam is not using speech to communicate but he can look to four corners of a page. His supporter wonders whether he knows the names of the animals in the book the group has been listening to. She copies the pictures of the animals in different poses and sticks them in four corners of a sheet.
>
> She asks Sam: 'Can you show me the cat? Can you show me the one sitting down? Which one is furthest away from the tree? Which is being active? Which one is making a noise?'
>
> Sam can answer all the questions showing that although he cannot speak he has been listening and is able to understand the story and communicate this very well.

Children with cerebral palsy enjoy listening to stories and, like all children, they need to see themselves represented in the stories they are told (see www.childreninthepicture.org.uk). Children with cerebral palsy can enjoy reading, particularly stories they recognise and are familiar with. There are some points to note:

- Most children with cerebral palsy are better served by a whole word and whole phrase approach as they have great difficulty shaping the sounds for phonics.
- Some children with visual difficulties will need a lot of practice and support to maintain a left to right direction with their eyes. Games following cars or a ball rolling or a torch beam can help.
- Computer programs that link words and phrases together and have a read-back facility such as Clicker (see page 82) are really helpful at this point and can enable a child to bank words and phrases with the help of a supporter to link together and be read out by the computer giving the child a voice.

This type of program is also very useful for writing. They are important because:

- Some children with cerebral palsy may never have sufficient muscular control to tackle the ever increasing demands on their writing skills as they move through school. It can be difficult for an early years setting to recognise this but if the child is having difficulty with the everyday hand tasks then these are not likely to go away as demands increase.
- All children with cerebral palsy are hugely advantaged by early and regular access to a computer and practise to scan and select words and phrases from banks they choose with their supporter.

All children will want to attempt aspects of handwriting but many will never get beyond making marks with a broad felt tip pen and may always relay on IT for this. For those where handwriting is considered appropriate there are a variety of aids available:

- Most children will benefit from a writing slope. This is usually a wooden or Perspex wedge that sets the paper at an angle of about 45 degrees, however a large lever arch file can be used to try this out with the child to see if it is helpful.

- A fatter softer pen grip once they start to use a pen.
- They should not use pencil as this requires more grip and far more down-force causing more fatigue and pain.
- Using a Dycem mat to stop the paper slipping (see page 82) or Blu tack to anchor paper will help. This is particularly important for children with hemiplegia as they have difficulty using the weaker hand to anchor their work.

You should check the best support for the child with their occupational therapist. As a general rule children with cerebral palsy benefit from getting into a good sitting position:

- The child may need to fix one hand on a grip in order to use the other. See the Rifton catalogue for grab bars and arm supports to help in this. Ask the child's occupational therapist what is best. http://www.rifton.com/products/sitting/armanchors/AnchorFamily.html
- Feet flat, bottom back, with ankles, knees and hips as close to right angles as possible is usually the desired position.
- Feet need to be firmly on the ground, so for some children we need to use a solid flat foot rest to give this stability. Using a box or a telephone directory can give the right support.
- Head, hands and trunk in the middle of the child's body and facing forward. Repositioning throughout the task is usually necessary.

Problem Solving, Reasoning and Numeracy

Some children with cerebral palsy only have access issues when exploring number and problem solving. Others will have the neurological difficulties that are part of the brain repair work that went on before and soon after they were born. With very young children it may be difficult to know whether the problems are just about access to the activities or whether the child is going to need a great deal of help in this area.

The child will need to use numbers as labels and for counting. It is likely that many children with cerebral palsy will be delayed in this area and will not yet have developed a good understanding of number in terms of labelling groups or counting, except as a rhyme.

- The child is likely to need a great deal of practical experiences of number, with numbers being attached to familiar items - one shoe two shoes, one hand two hands, etc.

60

- Using rhyme and story and giving the child the chance to choose two, rather than one, of a favourite toy can help.

- The child may or may not have the communication skills to recite numbers but could choose the one that 'comes next' in a short sequence through looking towards or pointing to the correct picture or group of objects.
- There is always a way to include the child with cerebral palsy, whatever the level of need. For example when playing action games where children move towards the finish line according to the number of steps they take the child with cerebral palsy could be the caller or show a numbered card. When children are building a tower from blocks the child with cerebral palsy may not have the hand control to place blocks but could choose the colour or shape, or could tell his friends to place one, two or three blocks at a time - using voice or cards.

For some children, even at three or four years of age, they may still have difficulty understanding concepts or calculating quantities such as more or less. Their appreciation of bigger and smaller may still be related to tallness and their understanding of removing one from a group may be limited to 'gone'. Careful observation is critical to ensure that the child is offered activities at an appropriate level with the targets set being achievable.

- Offering groups of desirable objects such as toys or treats can quickly tell us if the child goes for the larger amount and has an understanding of group size.
- Playing the 'gone' game (where a child has to remember the items on a tray and tell which has been taken away) can not only improve visual memory but also tell us if they actually know one is missing.
- If the child does not have good spoken communication, play matching objects to pictures, then use the pictures to allow the child to indicate which is 'gone' from a choice of two.
- Sharing is a good way of dividing up quantities with a group of children.
- With any new skill or concept, it is important to continue with the activity with different objects over a longer time to establish learning and revisit this regularly even when you begin to teach a new skill.

Having four objects and sharing in different ways through saying, 'One for me, one for him and two for her' is a good way to practise this skill.

Many children will have difficulty understanding that the *total number* remains the same, so it is important to have a base with the pictures of the objects in the middle of the group and return them to this base to check the number is still the same.

Children with cerebral palsy do not have the same opportunities to move in space, handle shapes or use their bodies to measure items. Around 60% of children with cerebral palsy will also have difficulties associated with the repair work in their brain having used up vital parts of the visual processing areas particularly necessary for this type of learning. To overcome these difficulties the child will need to:

- physically move through space and explore objects as much as possible. This means coming out of secure seating and rolling around on the floor.
- reach and touch as many shapes, sizes and textures as possible.

The child will need to post shapes but may not be able to physically pick up and handle a shape, rotate it and manoeuvre it into a matching recess or posting hole. You could:

- glue small wooden knobs to large inset jigsaws with only a few pieces;
- use a colourful biscuit tin that rattles as the object drops in;
- use fingerless mittens with Velcro, sewn to the mittens and stuck to small objects, so that the child can reach into containers and get objects.

However some children may need to work at a much more basic level and play the game 'Will my chair fit into your lunch box?'. This is an exciting game for all the children so makes it easy to include the child in a group.

The game takes a series of boxes familiar to the child and goes through the pantomime of asking the question if various familiar objects could fit in. Whatever answer the child gives we go through the motions of trying to fit the objects into the boxes and either agree with the child or demonstrate the impossibility of their answer. As the child gets familiar with the game we introduce more subtle differences moving towards matching shapes and sizes.

Knowledge and Understanding of the World

Many children with cerebral palsy will have a more limited and very different experience of the world around them. Some will know a great deal about hospitals and treatments and may seem old beyond their years when discussing their difficulties. Some have a great fear of people in white coats. Some who are tube fed may never have experienced tastes and textures of foods and others who cannot walk may have limited knowledge of up and down or distance or time. It is important not to take for granted the level of knowledge children come to your setting with and we need to observe carefully whether the child has understanding about his world at the same level as his other abilities.

Setting the scene for children with cerebral palsy to explore and investigate needs careful thinking. Every play activity offers opportunities:

- If the child is playing in water they can fill and pour and drop and float or sink if they have use of their hands.
- If they are relying on a supporter they can request actions or show anticipation or interest in the actions they are supported to undertake.
- They can investigate the properties of flour and dough or wet and dry sand.
- They can choose what to stick onto paper or objects.
- They can predict if things will dissolve or remain whole.
- They can go out into the garden and collect leaves and twigs and contribute to making a nest for the wall display.

Similarly with designing and making:

- They can contribute to the general planning as part of a group.
- They can help knock things down and enjoy and anticipate the experience.
- They can choose components, colours and materials and take an interest in the finished product.
- They can choose colours and direct lines in artwork and be assisted to create splatter patterns.

ICT could be the area where they really shine:

- Early and regular access to computers with the right access and software can ensure that their skills are easy to see and noticed and highly regarded by the whole team.
- Start with switch operated toys and talking books and move on to cause

and effect programs on the computer.

- Give the child a great deal of practice to enable her to operate a switch and support plenty of activities to help the child scan and select on computer games with inbuilt rewards.
- Using gel pads, switches, joysticks or tracker ball, ask the IT adviser to slow down the response time on the preferred interface so that the child's tremor and spasm are equalled out as far a possible. The inclusion team in your local authority may have an advisor to help or if you purchase the device from a store they may have a helpdesk that would do this for you.

- If the child does not have hand control ask for a specialist assessment for switching as the child may be able to use a foot, chin or shoulder switch with the right equipment and training. The child's speech and language therapist could pursue this.

Praise, fun and lots of practice will give the child the best possible opportunity.

The concept of time can present considerable difficulty for children with ccerebral palsy. They have more limited experiences of time and may have a body clock where the rhythms of their waking and sleeping are out of time with the rest of their family and the other children in the group.

- Time also depends heavily on association of activities with particular times and the child's short life may have been a round of appointments and visits by professionals that have disrupted all reasonable attempts to provide a routine in the home.
- Around one in four children with cerebral palsy experiences anxiety. Sudden changes in activity can cause huge distress resulting in crying or tantrum behaviours. Provide these children with a picture time line.
- Use counting down from activities with reminders of what will happen next. These can ease anxiety and allow the child to begin to associate times and actions.
- The use of familiar songs to indicate activities can also be a great help.

Children with cerebral palsy may have difficulty with spatial awareness and have little idea of the relationship between places.

- Those children who are walking are concentrating on the walking rather than the spaces they travel along.

- Those that are being carried or pushed may be more concerned with the person or speed of the travel than where they are going.
- Placing clear indicators such as pictures relating to each area in the setting can help establish a sense of place.
- When travelling to a place inside or outside the building show the child points along the way and tell him that you are getting nearer to the place. As the child learns these markers you can start to help him anticipate where the group is going to.
- For trips into the community build an expectation of what you will meet along the way through story and pictures before going. Use these pictures to support a sense of travelling to a place as you go along.

You have already done a great deal to foster a sense of community through the toys, wall displays and story books the children have encountered:
- Like all the other children, the child with cerebral palsy will enjoy bringing in pictures of family and home.
- It is equally important to share the child's culture and customs through pictures and objects.

Physical Development

Whether walking independently, using a walker or a chair, all children with cerebral palsy will have difficulty with physical development. It is very important for them to experience lots of independent movement. This creates associations and pathways in the brain that underpin learning essential for the development of mathematics, time, and other necessary skills.

For the child with cerebral palsy to experience movement in space you will need to think about the organisation of spaces. Some possible ideas are:
- Partition off a corner with moveable cupboards and cover this surface with padded mats so that crawling, shuffling and rolling can take place in safety.
- Rather than sitting on a chair or in a corner seat for story time the child could lie on a mat and wriggle about while listening.
- Children with hemiplegia will benefit from three wheeled push-along bikes that promote safe wobble in order to ensure they use their weaker side.

- Music and movement sessions can involve lying and rolling as well as standing and stepping.
- There are many small battery vehicles for children from as young as nine months that allow the child to operate a touch switch and make the vehicle move. These can give a first taste of independent movement. The child's physiotherapist or occupational therapist can advise on suitability.

All small children need to have their health and bodily awareness taken care of in the setting:
- Children with cerebral palsy often have difficulty sleeping and may need rest periods.
- Children with constantly moving muscles or those with very tight muscles often need twice as much food to grow and stay healthy as others and have difficulty eating enough at one sitting.
- All children with cerebral palsy experience more pain and fatigue.
- Ensure the setting provides an oasis (quiet space) where the child can spend quiet times or have an additional snack.
- Talk to the family about sending in high energy snacks.

Many young children with cerebral palsy may have difficulty tolerating food with lumps, unfamiliar textures and tastes. You will need to give them lots of opportunities to try different foods in a fun environment but the overriding responsibility is to make sure the child gets sufficient food to stay healthy. This may mean that a 'healthy' snack for a child with cerebral palsy may be high calorie. Try these:
- If the child only eats one type of food offer other snacks when he is hungry.
- Without any fuss give the child the liked food as soon as the new food is touched or gets near the mouth or the child accepts a tiny taste.
- Do lots of food play with sticky foods like icing sugar or dough and dry foods such as dried beans and lentils (NB. check for food allergies).
  See *Food Talks* published by Scope for more ideas.

Many children with cerebral palsy need help with personal care. For some this will be a lifelong need.
- Teach the child the names of body parts, having first discussed the way the family names them.

- For the child without speech, provide pictures large enough for the child to indicate parts of the body so that he can tell you if something is wrong. For example pointing to the tummy and then to an emotion card for hungry.

Children with cerebral palsy will need a great deal of adult support when using equipment and materials.

- Children may stay at the sensory stage for longer and get pleasure from making patterns in sand with their hands or feet or in drawing their hands through poster paint thickened with cornflour.
- Hand eye coordination for many children with cerebral palsy will be bringing both hands together, and some children with athetosis will have great difficulty co-ordinating hands and eyes.
- For one child in the group coordination will be building a high tower of bricks, but for the child with cerebral palsy it may be in moving a hand to knock it down.

Here are some items that will help the child with cerebral palsy to achieve some use of equipment and materials:

- Magnet boards set on a writing slope can allow some children to move them around to achieve patterns or pictures.
- Stickle bricks may be combined as part of building as they cling together once they touch.
- Using balls or cylinders to create patterns. The child could move along the floor to push them into place and the resulting pattern could be photographed.
- Some children with better hand use maybe able to use Lego or other blocks. Some will use large Lego and others small depending how well they can use their hands.

Children with ataxia will be able to bring their hands to the midline and manipulate equipment but will need to bring these close to their body to keep control. Children with athetoid cerbral palsy will not be able to repeat actions easily so they will need a variety of requests or be encouraged to work out their own solutions to situations.

The main equipment for children with cerebral palsy will be touch or switch operated toys and the computer. With these they will be able to explore the world more easily and fully, and gain control over their environment. Toy libraries can sometimes lend individual children these toys and many toys can be easily adapted for switch use.

You can ask for help locally or follow the simple instructions on this website and try to adapt toys yourselves: http://www.ataccess.org/resources/wcp/enswitches/enadaptingtoy.html See also www.stepscharity.org/ for individual loan of toys and switch devices to families by post.

Jenny loves the Jack in the Box toy so staff asked the local further education college electrical engineering department if they could make a switch for her to operate it herself. They took a few weeks to fit the request in but when it came back she was delighted.

Creative Development

Many children with cerebral palsy will be full of ideas and burning with the desire to express themselves. Providing good access is hugely important to enable them to express their ideas and feelings. For others there can be a reluctance to step outside what is familiar and they will need encouragement and time to participate in sensory experiences outside their comfort zone.

To support children in being creative we need to provide a large number of sensory experiences.

- **Sensory boxes** can be put together for very small amounts of money and can be enjoyed by all the children in the group.
- Simple items such as **natural sponges or nylon body scrubbers, emery boards and holographic wrapping paper** can be used to provide a range of experiences that can form part of the child's daily routine. Treasure baskets are invaluable and publications such as the *Little Book of Treasure Baskets*, Featherstone Education, and others in the *Little Books* series provide lots of good ideas.
- These activities can be table based but are equally possible on the floor in a lying position or propped over a wedge and can be shared with others in the group.
- Where the child does not have clear speech the activity should be supported with **picture or symbol cards** or, for some children who have reasonable hand use, by signing. Most children with cerebral palsy are not well supported by signing as while it may help them understand it will not help those with poor hand control to express themselves.

- The child can express their creativity through making choices.
- ICT with appropriate software and switches can help the child build a picture and show how good their imagination and planning can be.

There are many opportunities for expression through music:
- Strap bells to wrists or ankles.
- Use clappers or bells on the end of short poles to encourage grasp and release.
- Touch pad sound makers can help the children express themselves through music.

The child will need support exploring media and materials - some of these ideas may help:
- Cut a hole in a sock to help the child get one finger extended for finger painting or using the fist or whole hand can be successful for the child who has relaxed muscles and has difficulty making a fist.
- Put blobs of coloured paint on paper and let the child roll a ball or toy car through them.
- Pad the handle of a paintbrush with foam for a better grip.
- Put glue onto paper and give the child a hand shaped small yoghurt pot with a plastic bag for a lid. Pull the bag tightly across the top and fasten with a rubber band. Make a hole or holes in this lid for the sprinkles to come through - sand, glitter, rice, etc.
- Scissors are difficult - try spring loaded squeezy scissors or use double grip scissors that the adult can support .

If the child has vision problems ensure that:
- there is a good contrast with light coloured materials against a plain dark background;
- the light is not glaring or reflecting strongly off the surface;
- there are different textures available to support vision through touch.

Using contrasting shapes to support choosing:
- Place the items to be explored in a shallow tray to prevent them from moving away.
- Name the items the child touches as the exploration goes on.
- Encourage the child to handle many different shapes and textures.

The child will enjoy joining in with activities creating music and dance:
- Music can be created through touch pads or banging and shaking.

- There are many creative ICT music programs the child could use as part of group activities.
- Some children with cerebral palsy react very strongly to certain pitches and sounds and many have a 'startle reflex' that puts their body into spasm when surprised by movement or sound. If the child has this you may need to start the joining in from a distance, where the child can get physical and verbal reassurance that the sound is not threatening.
- Some children outgrow this reflex and are able to accept a level of unexpected sounds, for others it is part of their lifelong disability and they may have to experience a quieter programme of sounds away from the general group.
- You may find other children in the group would also prefer a gentler approach. These children could make ideal play partners in this activity for the child with cerebral palsy.

Most children enjoy developing imagination and imaginative play and only need support to facilitate their involvement.

- If they have clear speech they will often take a lead role although much of their early play can reflect the medical knowledge they have.
- Where the child does not have clear speech it is important that they have a means of communication with their group as well as with their supporter.
- A supporter could help the child decide what they wanted to be and help the child get into the costume but should then withdraw and let play develop. These are things to watch out for:
  - Are the other children responding appropriately to the role the child is playing?
  - Is the child using expressions of face or body or vocalising showing participation?
  - Are other children taking over the child and treating him as younger or as an object?

The supporter may need to step in and redirect the play if the child is being treated as a much younger member of the group or being monopolised by one motherly child. Some children need many experiences to build an imaginative picture of their world. These children may show other difficulties with interaction and communication. They may need pictures and objects to help them take an imaginative journey into a fantasy world. Try using story sacks.

As the child progresses with IT skills she can participate with others in building storylines through using her computer grids.

Look listen and note: observing, assessing and recording

Observation and assessment, formal and informal are central to the EYFS. When a child has cerebral palsy the way they tackle playing and learning may look different and the child may not always be able to demonstrate their participation clearly. In the light of these differences we need to consider how we observe and record their progress. Children with cerebral palsy present themselves in a wide variety of different ways so the ideas given here can only be general and you will need to think carefully about they ways observation and assessment can support the child you have in your group.

Remember when observing and assessing all children to make a note of the following:

- time of day;
- who is interacting with the child;
- context (e.g. in a group or on their own);
- any other factors (not well, tired, before or after food, etc.).

Write down what you see. We call this **outcome recording**.

- Describe what you *see* not what you think it means. For example, if the child is smiling when playing write down, 'Chloe smiled when playing in the sand' *NOT* 'Chloe was happy to play in the sand'.
- Revisit the observations each week to see if patterns emerge. This is important, as you may find that she smiles and interacts well after food but cries and doesn't make eye contact in the 45 minutes before food. You might then offer a high calorie snack halfway through the morning and see if this improves her outcomes.

Three examples of outcome recording

Danny is playing with toy cars in a group of three children. He is lying propped up over a rolled towel and has his hands forward. He plays for around 15 minutes before showing signs of fatigue.

Outcome Record	
Child	Danny (3 yrs 4 months). Monday 10.09.07
Environment	lying – propped over roll (with St, G)
Activity	car play with St and G
Outcome	Uses left hand mainly to manipulate car. Frequently looks up at G and smiles. Screeches when St removes car, smiles when G returns car to him. Uses right hand to push car back to left hand. Follows St with eyes as he leaves the group and smiles when he returns with more cars. Makes GGGG noise as G rolls cars towards him. (5 minute observation. Play lasted about 15 minutes)
Observer	JB (Key Person)

The following week JB is again observing Danny

Outcome Record	
Child	Danny (3yrs 4 months). Tuesday 18.09.07
Environment	table – supported seating (with grab bar)*
Activity	car inset jigsaw with G, Am and Al.
Outcome	Uses left hand to manipulate pieces. Reminded by his supporter at intervals of about 2 mins to return his right hand to the grab bar. Frequently looks up at G and smiles. Grabs large inset piece by knob and bangs on table. Startles himself and extends backwards. His supporter (TM) speaks soothingly and massages his hand. Extension relaxes in 2 mins and Danny returns to grabbing inset piece. TM taps the inset shape that corresponds to the piece in his hand. Danny looks at the recess and makes several movements to connect. TM steadies his arm from behind giving support at the upper arm and moving board into a better position. Danny pushes the shape into the recess. TM draws attention to his actions. G claps. Al and Am join in. Danny smiles and tries to grab another piece. (9 minute observation, play lasted about 14 minutes)

* Grab bar: a bar fixed to the table to help Danny maintain his balance by grasping it firmly with one hand as he uses the other hand to play.

Smita is spending some time with her age group. The team are gradually transferring her to the older group. Her new Key Person is observing to get to know her.

Outcome Record	
Child	Smita (2yrs 4 months). Monday 10.09.07
Environment	home corner – in supported seat
Activity	house play with Ga, F and Z
Outcome	Looks around. Chews on fist. Follows Z with her eyes as Z takes the parent role. Accepts a cup from F. Bangs the cup. Makes grizzling sound. Gr pats her hand. Stops grizzling. F hands her a plastic sandwich. Smita puts it to her mouth. Z asks Smita if the sandwich tastes good. Smita smiles. (6 minute observation, play lasted about 8 minutes)
Observer	HR (Key Person)

We might want to make more formal assessments. Scope has developed some simple graphic based assessments. These provide simple picture pages with from four to 180 pictures on an A4 sheet. Through playing 'look and find' games with these sheets the size of picture that the child can access becomes clear. (Contact earlyyears@scope.org.uk for a free CD.)

You can also make your own assessment materials. For example you might think that Ryu understands concepts such as: in, on, under, behind, on top, etc., but as he can't speak clearly you are not sure. Ryu responds really well to questions and gives a smile and a definite nod for 'Yes'. He has an equally definite look-away and frown for 'No'. You put two boxes on the table in front of him and put one toy teddy on top of the box and one identical teddy in the other box. You point to the box with the teddy INSIDE and say 'Teddy is IN the box' and to the other and say 'Teddy in ON the box'. You take both out and place a teddy ON one box. You ask Ryu, 'Ryu, is Teddy IN the box?' You expect a 'No' response. On another occasion you can ask a question and expect a 'Yes' response. Once you establish this as a way of assessing you can extend it to many other areas of learning.

Planning and differentiation

Planning and differentiation for children with cerebral palsy is part of setting out their Individual Education plan (IEP) and can take a variety of different forms. There are different ways to access such as:

- larger formats;
- items placed on a sloping surface to aid looking;
- use magnets and Velcro;
- gloves with items attached by Velcro to maintain grasp for longer;
- songs to cue activities.

Different ways to respond to resources such as:

- looking and smiling;
- hand movements;
- vocalising with different tones;
- tolerating - child endures a disliked activity for a short time;
- accepting - child allows the activity to happen without much protest but does not show any signs of engagement;
- enjoying - activity is initiated by the practitioner and the child shows signs of enjoyment through smiling, relaxing or other means but is not making any efforts to get involved;
- participating - child is actively attempting to engage with the activity through vocalisation, body movement etc;
- innovating - child is active in getting the practitioner to start the activity through vocalising, looking intently, drawing attention to what she wants.

Adapted and differentiated resources:

- Stick a sponge tab to the edges of early card books to enable page turning.
- Stick small drawer knobs to large inset jigsaw pieces.
- Adapt toys so they can be switch operated.
- Use electronic voices through a switch or talking device.

Taking ideas from earlier developmental stages:

- Children with cerebral palsy may have ideas that are age appropriate but may only be able to demonstrate understanding at a much earlier developmental level. Be prepared to look back to very early developmental stages to find appropriate ideas for activities.

Dylan has quadriplegic cerebral palsy. He is 26 months old and goes to a childminder four days a week. He laughs and smiles a lot and really enjoys stories. He loves the company of Jenny, who is 30 months. Jenny is beginning to recognise numbers and often holds up fingers saying 'one' and 'two'. The childminder is keen to explore number rhymes with both children and Jenny enjoys counting games. When playing with the children together they both have number rhymes and counting games, Jenny demonstrates her abilities through counting to five, and Dylan demonstrates his through his anticipation of the rhymes and by pointing to his eyes with the song 'One Nose, One Mouth, Two (pause while Dylan points) Eyes and a Chinny, Chin, Chin.' (to the tune of 'The Big Ship Sails on the Ally Ally O'). This response is more appropriate for a child of 8-20 months, but he is showing the beginning of understanding the number 2 through his actions.

The format the IEP takes will be different in different settings and your Area SENCo will advise on the formats used locally. The IEP should have three to five targets. To write the IEP we ask the question: 'What is it really important for this child to learn?' When we know what the most important things are we can work them into all our planning activity.

Example of an IEP for Raj (drawn up working together with parents, physiotherapist and SENCo)

Raj needs to use his right hand to grasp and release:

- Raj will take part in activities that encourage flat hands with extended fingers, holding and letting go and fixing one hand using a grab bar while he does these.
- Raj will express his preferences and opinions.
- Raj will take part in activities that offer choices. He will be asked if he likes or dislikes activities and his preferences will be acted upon.

Raj needs to extend his finger to point:

- Raj will be given a warm water hand bath at the beginning of the morning and afternoon sessions.
- Following this he will be given activities that encourage extending his index finger (right hand).

Raj needs to tolerate group activities:

- Raj will be included in small group activities.
- Activities will include a lot of singing which he likes.
- Time spent in group activities will be extended to 10 minutes over the course of three months.

In this example Mary and Raj both have additional needs. Mary has severe learning difficulties and Raj has cerebral palsy (see his IEP above). The group leader has planned a practical activity making a flower book with the group. She has looked at the IEPs for Mary and Raj and makes sure the children practice parts of the IEP relevant to this activity.

Sample Activity Plan
Group: sunflower - making a flower book

	Individual solutions
Song "What shall we do with our hands today?" (patting table with hands).	
'Round and round the garden' (rolling ball with flat hands.	Mary will tolerate hand patting on the table with hand over hand (where the practitioner places her hand over Mary's hand to take Mary through the movements required).
'Two little flowers sitting on a wall' (grasp rods with flower pictures on).	Raj will maintain grasp with a full fist and look at flowers.
Singing to make the flower dance.	
Smell feel look at real flower.	Mary will vocalise back to her Supporter.
Talk about sun and rain needed to make flower grow.	Raj - 'says' if he likes or dislikes the experiences through nodding and smiling.
Show flower book – rhyme and hand actions.	Raj – 'says' rain or sunny at appropriate time through vocalisation.
'Flower flower growing high flower flower touch the sky flower flower wind whips round leaves and petals tumble down'.	Raj – picks out red, green, blue, yellow using a finger to point.
Colour pictures and stick in books.	both - encourage vocalisation of own name, then stick in books.
Show name labels and each child says their name and finds the name label to stick in books.	
Sing 'Mary Mary quite contrary, how does your garden grow?' to go with book	

Different approaches

In this book the focus has been on finding individual solutions to the challenges each child faces. However there are a number of different approaches you can use to support the child to access play and the EYFS curriculum.

Objects and miniatures

Some children, particularly those who are functioning at an early developmental stage, may not yet be ready to respond to pictures. However they may respond to familiar objects. We can use objects they know and recognise to help them make choices. We can build a vocabulary of objects children begin to recognise. We do this by always showing the same object every time the child gets a certain activity or food or drink.

The object is always shown first and the child given time to observe or handle it. The activity or reward (such as food or drink at snack time) follows immediately after showing the object. For example, the child is shown a beaker then given a sip of drink, or the child is shown an artificial flower then taken into the garden.

As children get more cued into this way of communicating the object can be more symbolic. The child is shown a toy car, signalling that he is going home in the car. The activities are a useful tool in helping children understand the world around them. They are taken from a system known as 'Objects of Reference'. The child's speech and language therapist should be able to advise if this is to become the child's communication system.

Pictures, symbols and communication passports

Older children will be able to use pictures and symbols to share ideas and communicate. Catalogues are great sources of pictures of toys and everyday items the child will be familiar with. As part of a cutting and sticking activity the child can build a 'Communication Passport'. This is a simple, child centred document that sets out things a child likes and dislikes and how they can communicate with others. It may contain a mix of family and group photos of the child playing with siblings and friends and pictures generated by a computer or cut out of a catalogue.

The pictures are all chosen by the child and it can take days or weeks to build. Other children in the group will want to build their own communication passports so it can be a group activity. If you are using a digital camera to record activities these pictures are really useful in keeping a communication passport up to date. If you are looking for pictures on particular topics Google images offer lots of ideas.

As the child has more to say he will need to move to a more formal system, perhaps using symbols. These are generally computer based and commercially available. Two easy to use systems are Clicker 5 and Widgit (see page 82 and 83 for details). These systems are excellent tools to help young children learn. These can be used to create labels and information cards for story and play corners. As the child's need for a more complex communication system grows they can be used to create communication boards or books where the child keeps the symbols in regular use and can access them easily. The child's speech and language therapist will advise on the suitability of a communication book or chart.

At this stage it is important that everyone at home and in the early years settings is using pictures and symbols, not just the child with cerebral palsy. When choosing activities or drink the pictures and symbols are shown to everyone in the group.

Another really good use for symbols with the whole group is supporting children to recognise and show emotions. The NSPCC have a useful resource 'how it is' which provides a large symbol vocabulary for helping children express emotions and stay safe. The materials are available from:

http://www.nspcc.org.uk/Inform/applications/HowItIs/index.asp

Gesture and signing

Giving good strong facial expressions, eye contact and body language cues are all really important in helping children understand. You can use a formal signing programme such as Makaton (www.makaton.org/) or Signalong (www.signalong.org.uk/wa/). Both these systems have been developed for slightly different groups from the British Sign Language for the Deaf (BSL). A signing system is good for supporting language and communication skills in all children but it can have limited application for children with cerebral palsy that affects their arms or hands.

Switches and buttons

If the child with cerebral palsy can learn to use a switch or button operated device early on and see that they can make things happen, they will be on the road to being able to access the curriculum, play and communication. Early access to switch activated toys then computer programs gives the child the motivation to interact with the world around. Finding the right switch can be time consuming but it is worth persevering. The child's speech and language therapist should be able to support this. Toy libraries may be able to lend switch operated toys to families or the local pre-school support service may have a loan bank. Families can also access the free postal switch operated toys service from www.stepscharity.org/.

Helping the child with cerebral palsy on the path to reading

Children with cerebral palsy can learn to read but are often unable to articulate the words clearly to read aloud. Some have very good visual skills and good visual memory and can often remember and point to short phrases associated with everyday events. Using the Etran frame (see pages 31 and 83) the child can indicate the correct word or phrase by eye pointing to the word or words stuck with Blu-tack to each corner of the frame. Start with the child's own name and the names of other children in the group. They can picture and word match and they can also play word and picture bingo. Scope has a free CD with ideas to promote reading for children with poor speech and poor use of their hands (see page 82). Learning, recognising and remembering a whole word and short phrase will give the child a great deal of confidence to tackle reading later on.

The EYFS framework emphasises the importance of phonics. Practitioners looking into the guidance will find nothing about alternative approaches for children with difficulties forming letter shapes, sounds and words. Phonics are an essential part of reading fluently but the child who has difficulty forming sounds is gravely disadvantaged if this is the only approach used. Whole word recognition can be used alongside the phonic activities provided and can provide success for a child who cannot engage fully with the phonic approach. Story based phonic approaches such as Letterland (http://www.letterland.com/) can support the child with cerebral palsy to begin to learn to recognise the sounds that go with letter shapes, even if they cannot vocalise them.

Most children love rhyme and rhythm and these will help them as learning gets more formal. The pace and tempo of familiar children's rhymes can provide a safe and motivating start for children to attempt sounds and words that they find impossible to produce in isolation. Rhythm and familiar rhymes support children with cerebral palsy to move and respond at a comfortable tempo.

Signposting and contacts

For your bookshelf:

Miller & Bachrach: *Cerebral palsy - a complete guide to caregiving*. John Hopkins University Press. ISBN 9780801883552,

Stanton M: *Cerebral palsy handbook - a practical guide for parents and carers*. Vermillion. ISBN 0091876761

Martin S: *Teaching motor skills to children with cerebral palsy and similar movement disorders. – a guide for parents and professionals*. Woodbine House. ISBN 1890627720

National Children's Bureau: *The dignity of risk - practical handbook for professionals working with disabled children and their families*. NCB. ISBN 1904787223

Useful contacts and organisations

Bobath Centre. Tel: 020 8444 3355 Email: info@bobathlondon.co.uk www.bobath.org.uk/

Capability Scotland – for people with cerebral palsy. Advice line: 0131 313 5510 Email: ascs@capability-scotland.org.uk/ www.capability-scotland.org.uk

Cerebra - for brain injured children and young people. www.cerebra.org.uk/

Contact a Family. Helpline: 0808 808 3555 Email: info@cafamily.org.uk www.cafamily.org.uk

Early Support. Builds on existing good practice in partnership with families who use services and the many agencies that provide services for young children. www.earlysupport.org.uk

Epilepsy Action. Helpline: 0808 800 5050 Email: helpline@epilepsy.org.uk www.epilepsy.org.uk

ERIC – Education & Resources for Improving Childhood Continence. Tel: 0117 960 3060 Email: info@eric.org.uk www.eric.org.uk

Face2Face (Scope) - Parent to Parent befriending. Tel: 0844 800 9189 Email: face2facenetwork@scope.org.uk www.face2facenetwork.org.uk

The Foundation for Conductive Education. Tel: 0121 449 1569 Email: info@conductive-education.org.uk www.conductive-education.org.uk

HemiHelp - for people with hemiplegia. Tel: 0845 120 3713. Email: support@hemihelp.org.uk Web: www.hemihelp.org.uk

Makaton Vocabulary Development Project (MVDP). Tel: 01276 61 390 Email: mvdp@makaton.org www.makaton.org

National Parent Partnership Network. Information on finding local parent partnership services.   www.parentpartnership.org.uk/

NSPCC - safeguarding children. This charity produces a useful CD of emoticons called 'How it is'. www.nspcc.org.uk

Scope - about cerebral palsy - equality for disabled people. Response helpline: 0808 800 3333. Email: response@scope.org.uk   www.scope.org.uk

Sense - for people with multiple sensory impairments. Tel: 0845 127 0060. Textphone: 0845 127 0062. Email: info@sense.org.uk.   www.sense.org.uk

United Cerebral Palsy. An American organisation that provides information and advice for people with cerebral palsy, their parents and carers. The website has recent research and information sheets to download. www.ucp.org

Resources

Chairs - there are a number of sources for different types of robust chairs that give good support. Look at:
    www.rifton.com
    www.smirthwaite.co.uk/index.html
    www.nrs-uk.co.uk/ProductDetails.aspx?Material=G87261

Clicker - a computer programme that staff can use to produce symbols for labelling around the room and allows a child to use a computer to communicate, also supports pre-school literacy. Find out more from: http://www.cricksoft.com/uk/products/clicker/

Continence

Scope has a fact sheet 'Coming out of nappies', which contains more information www.scope.org.uk

For specific advice about continence, you can contact the Continence Foundation Nurse Helpline. Tel 0845 345 0165 www.continence-foundation.org.uk

You can also call National Action on Incontinence. Tel 01536 533 255. www.incontact.org

Doidy cup - a plastic, two handed beaker with a sloping top that enables a child to take very small sips. Available from: www.nctsales.co.uk/prodshow.asp?id=750

Dycem - a rubbery plastic mat that clings on both sides and can be used to stop things slipping such as paper on a table or the child's feet when trying to achieve a good sitting position. Different sizes can be obtained from: http://onlineshop.rnib.org.uk

Etran frame - a Perspex oblong with hand-holds that can be held up between practitioner and child, to offer the child choices from pictures placed in its corners. Information is available from the CALL centre (a communication charity) http://callcentre.education.ed.ac.uk/. Available from: cec.co@lineone.net.

Food Talks - a file of information about early eating and drinking difficulties and ideas to make eating fun. Available from: earlyyears@scope.org.uk

Go Talk 4+ - A lightweight portable communication aid that can pre-record 16 messages plus 'yes' and 'no'. Available from: http://www.inclusive.co.uk/catalogue/acatalog/go_talk_4.html

Mirrors - safe stand alone mirrors can be obtained from: www.smirthwaite.co.uk/index.html

Reading activity pack - this has been developed to support the earliest signs of reading ability – looking, to demonstrating reading without using speech. It therefore suits a wide range of ages and abilities. To get a copy please contact earlyyears@scope.org.uk and request the Scope Inclusion CD.

Two wheeled push along bikes - these 'learn to balance' bikes can be obtained from Bright Minds: http://www.brightminds.co.uk

Widget - a computer programme that staff can use to produce symbols for labelling around the room and also supports pre-school literacy. Find out more from: www.widgit.com.

Important words simply explained

ataxic - a form of cerebral palsy that affects balance

athetoid or **dyskinetic** - a form of cerebral palsy that affects the flow of movement in the whole body and can look jerky or writhing

communication aids - this describes a wide variety of ways a child can be supported to communicate and ranges from simple pictures drawn on paper to sophisticated electronic speech synthesizers

communication passport - a simple document that captures the important things about how the child communicates and what he likes and dislikes

diplegia - a form of cerebral palsy that affects just two limbs (usually both legs)

dycem - a rubbery plastic mat that stops items slipping

eye pointing - a way of communicating through looking towards pictures or objects and making choices or giving information

hemiplegia - a form of cerebral palsy that affects one side of the body

hypertonia - where the muscles are too tight; sometimes called 'high muscle tone'

hypotonia - where the muscles are too relaxed; sometimes called 'floppy'

Makaton - a way of communicating and supporting understanding using signing

neurodisability - a physical, learning or behaviour difficulty that happens because of something going wrong in the brain

spasticity - a form of cerebral palsy where the muscles tighten but do not relax properly

Signalong - a way of communicating and supporting understanding using signing

spatial awareness - the way a child interprets information about where she is in space, in relation to other people and objects. A child with spatial awareness difficulties may be clumsy and bump into things

spasm - where the muscle groups tighten instantly causing twisting of limbs or arching of the back; rather like extreme cramp

quadriplegia - where the cerebral palsy affects all four limbs.

Disability Discrimination Act and early years settings

The Disability Discrimination Act (DDA) has applied to the way childcare settings provide goods and services since 1996. In 2001 the act was amended to include education, and since 2002 this has meant that all the services offered in early years settings are covered by the act. The EYFS does not specifically mention the DDA but it encompasses the principles of non-discrimination in line with *Every Child Matters*.

Part 4 of the DDA applies to all schools, private or maintained, mainstream or special. Part 4 covers educational services including admissions and exclusions. Where discrimination may have occurred in a school setting and the complaint has not been resolved locally the complaint may be heard by the Special Educational Needs and Disabilities Tribunal (SENDisT).

Part 3 of the DDA applies to all early years settings that are not constituted as schools: day nurseries, playgroups, childminders and all voluntary fulltime and parttime provision. These duties cover goods and services such as refusing to provide a service, offering a lower standard or offering the service in worse terms. Settings that are not schools may still apply to the local authority for support in accepting a child with complex needs.

Two Key Duties that apply to both sections of the act:
* not to treat a disabled child less favourably
* to make reasonable adjustments.

What does the term 'disability' mean?

A child is considered disabled if the disability is long term (more than a year) and substantially affects the child's life.

What is meant by 'less favourable treatment'?

Less favourable treatment is when a child is treated less favourably than his or her non-disabled classmate. This less favourable treatment must be related directly to the child's disability.

What does 'justified' mean?

There are three areas where less favourable treatment can be justified. Where:
1. Entry criteria have been agreed that could discriminate.
2. It would involve unreasonable expenditure.
3. The setting could not reasonably know about the child's disability.

Can you give some examples?

An example of 'less favourable treatment' ... Gavin has a medical condition that means he has not acquired toilet training. His mother tries to enrol him in his local nursery only to be told that their policy requires all children to be out of nappies in order to attend. This policy discriminates against Gavin because his disability prevents him from being toilet-trained. This case, if it occurred in a school setting, could be heard at the SENDisT.

Examples of 'justification' ...

Richard has autism and his parents particularly like a local special school nursery. However, the school's entry criteria relate to children with physical disabilities and associated difficulties. The school is justified in not admitting Richard as he doesn't meet their entry criteria.

Jack has epilepsy and is on medication. Mum has not told anyone about the epilepsy or that the medication makes it difficult for him to concentrate. The nursery could not reasonably have known. However if Mum had told even one person at the nursery about his condition the responsibility of making that information known throughout the nursery would be on the nursery and not on the mother to make sure everyone knew.

What should an early years setting do to prevent discrimination happening?

Early years settings must:
1. Review their policies and practices to ensure that they do not discriminate against disabled children. This means that the setting with the policy about nappies, mentioned above, would have to change their policy and re-word it to one that made every attempt to overcome the difficulty with toilet hygiene for the child.
2. Plan to become increasingly inclusive not just for known children but for prospective children as well.
3. Make reasonable adjustments to the equipment and building.
4. Consider disabled children when they make changes to the environment or buy equipment or furniture.

Early years school settings do not have to:
1. buy any special equipment for the child.
2. employ any extra staff.
3. make any adaptations to their building. These should be provided through strategic planning or through the statement of special educational needs

if needed. Individual items are usually named in a child's statement but adaptations to the building have to be planned through long-term accessibility planning which is the responsibility of the local authority.

Services that are not schools are expected to make reasonable adjustments in line with affordability. For example a service that is physically inaccessible might not be expected to make physical alterations to the building but would be expected to consider other adjustments to service delivery such as changing the floor on which age groups were situated. These adjustments have to be reasonable and each situation is different.

DDA Helpline

The DDA Helpline provides a one-stop point for all your enquiries about the Disability Discrimination Act and employing disabled people. The Helpline number is 08457 622 633.

Further reading

Early Years and the Disability Discrimination Act 1995: what service providers need to know (published by the Council for Disabled Children), available from http://www.surestart.gov.uk/_doc/0-9E5AEC.pdf).

Disability Equality Duties (DED) (2006)

This legislation applies to public bodies. This means it applies directly to schools and school premises. However, as it applies to procurement as well as to in-house services, any setting receiving money from public bodies such as the local authority may be required to demonstrate how well they meet the requirements of the DDA. The DED requires schools, including their early years departments, to actively follow the duties under the DDA above and actively promote the welfare of disabled people. For more information visit http://www.teachernet.gov.uk/wholeschool/sen/disabilityandthedda/guidancedisabilityequalityinschools.